WHAT THEY ARE SAYING

From the village to the city and the world. That is the fascinating story of Emelia told in her lucid and inimitable style with no holds barred. A must-read for all ages. Engaging from start to finish.
Albert Fiadjoe, Professor

Perseverance is Dr. Timpo's compelling life story. It is not just a narrative of how Maa's little girl grew up to play with the big boys on the world stage. It gives us an insight into the social history of Ghana, the terrors of "working while black" in America and the challenges of a minority operator within the international civil service. Written in excellent easy prose, Emelia's candor and sincerity makes this book a page-turner.
Victor Essien, Rector & Professor of Law, Nyansapo College, Ghana & Principal, Law Office of Victor Essien, New York

This book is a rich collection of well documented memoirs, all beautifully woven together like a tapestry. The author takes pains to bring out the essence of perseverance in that journey. A great enchanting memoir worth reading!
Vicky Wireko-Andoh, Journalist/Columnist Daily Graphic, Ghana's leading newspaper

This book is a catechism for how to transform adversity to triumph. Emelia writes with aplomb. There is no life blemish that is smeared over, no subject that is taboo. This biography is a must-read for people of every background.
Louis Kofi Essandoh, MD, FACC, MedStar Heart and Vascular Institute

Story after compelling story unfolds as the author reveals, with endearing detail, her growing-up years in a small town in Ghana. Until she was 30, married with two children and a Ph.D., her horizons were limited only by her ambition and persistence. Then, because she was black and in the United States, many doors were slammed shut. How she succeeded, by reinventing herself at every turn, is a tale told with warmth, humor, and honesty.
Barbara Figge Fox, Journalist

A vivid picture of a rich life, with a rare window onto growing up in Ghana before Independence, through many peripatetic years in New York, Geneva, Rome, Namibia, Ethiopia, and other locales. Emelia has a sharp eye for detail and a loving view of her home country and its tapestry of cultures. This memoir memorializes one life, with its ups and downs, hard work, luck, and perseverance. I enjoyed seeing details of when our lives crossed paths and learning more about her earlier life.

Jessica Vapnek
Faculty Director, UC Law San Francisco

Dr. Emelia Timpo's book provides a front row seat to experience the life of one of Ghana's most accomplished international civil servants. From Kumasi, through Wesley Girls High School, Cornell and Rutgers, to a glittering UN career in Windhoek, Addis Ababa, Geneva and New York, Auntie Emelia has served the world with distinction. She and her beautiful family have every right to be proud of her achievements.

Dr. Victor Asare Bampoe,
Head, Global Programme Partnerships, UNAIDS

What a jewel and a masterpiece. It guides the inquisitive reader through a life journey with a humble beginning and passed through hills and valleys, crossed rivers, lakes, and mighty oceans and on this side of the Atlantic. It is certainly a must-read.

Prof. Kwaku Armah, retired educator

A riveting story that reflects the value inherent in the then Ghanaian educational system and the equally effective socialisation processes that have produced a selfless and hardworking international civil servant. A must read for all who are desirous of rekindling excellence and the can-do spirit among the youth, notably the girl child. *Ayekoo.*

Alexander Archine,
Managing Director, OAK Financial Services Limited and Dean,
Nyansapo College, Ghana.

PERSEVERANCE
A MEMOIR

ONE WOMAN'S JOURNEY FROM GHANA TO THE UNITED NATIONS & BEYOND

EMELIA TIMPO

ADINKRA
Publications

To Maa, a constant source of strength and love,
and to
Awoye, Emefa, Edem, and Albert who have enriched my life beyond
measure

A NOTE ON SPELLING

British English and American English are not always the same language. Spelling, in particular, changes from one country to another. I have, for the most part, used international or British spellings. I have tried for consistency throughout the book, but at times the spelling may switch from one style to another.

FOREWORD

When my wife, Kadija, delivered our first child in August 1992 in Brooklyn, New York, I had planned to be there but, due to the exigencies of my work, I was unable to travel at the time.

At very short notice, with a single phone call to Emelia, she and her husband, Albert Timpo, stood in for me, and brought my wife and the new baby home. A week later, in conformity with Ghanaian custom and tradition, they hosted, in their New Jersey home, a Moslem naming ceremony for our daughter, Shakira, with my family and friends in the United States in attendance.

One of our mutual friends, Daniel Aidoo Mensah, never ceases to repeat how he met the Timpos. He had lost all his travel documents at Geneva Airport and could not board his flight back to Accra after a business trip to Switzerland. Feeling disoriented and helpless, he contacted a gentleman he had met with earlier in the week. Knowing Daniel was a Ghanaian, he linked him up with Albert Timpo. He was sympathetic to Daniel's plight and went to the airport to bring him home. At home, Emelia and her daughter Emefa warmly received him, made him very comfortable and assured him every effort would be made to get new travel documents and flight bookings to return home. Indeed, she then contacted the Embassy of Ghana in Bern. He stayed with them for the week until Daniel's new passport was processed to enable his return to Accra.

I recount these two anecdotes as a teaser to the remarkable story of an incredibly generous and selfless lady whose autobiography you are about to read. It is a fascinating account of perseverance, humility, grit, "a can-do spirit," academic excellence, mother and child bonding and service to humanity through empathy for the underprivileged and marginalised. The book is also a testimony of faith, discipline, integrity and tolerance of diversity.

Emelia was not born with a silver spoon in her mouth. On the other hand, she was not born into poverty. After all, her mother was a certified midwife with her own practice in addition to owning a bakery, which supplied the leading Department stores in Kumasi. Her father held a Ph.D. and subsequently became the first Ghanaian Vice-Chancellor of one of the three universities in the country, the

University of Cape Coast.

The outstanding aspect of her childhood and upbringing, though, was through the towering role of her mother and many relatives, particularly the female role models and motivators who embedded her in a community of love, care and guidance. Emelia's mother placed a high premium on her education. She invested in sending her to boarding schools even at a very tender age. This laid a solid and sound foundation to assure Emelia's academic progression through highly competitive schools in later years. She attended Wesley Girls High School, Ghana's premier Girls Secondary School, the prestigious Kwame Nkrumah University of Science and Technology, the elite Ivy-league Cornell University and the renowned Rutgers University where she obtained a Ph.D. in Plant Physiology.

Another impressive feature running through the book is Emelia's humility. She has been a brilliant student throughout, either the best or always with the best in her class. And during her professional career, she has also been a high performer who goes beyond the call of duty to deliver on whatever she takes up. Yet she is far from boastful or engaging in self-praise. Rather, she constantly acknowledges and appreciates the support of her teachers, kind relatives, mentors, friends and colleagues who have contributed to her impressive success, in one way or the other, along the pathway of her life.

When reading these pages, one cannot but conclude that Emelia has led a truly fulfilling life. She seized every opportunity that came before her and made good use of it in a methodical and forward- thinking way. She planned carefully, applied herself diligently, did not look for short-cuts and earned the confidence, admiration and trust of all. In the process, she built a stable home, raised three beautiful children and made her mother, who had sacrificed so much for her, proud of her achievements in her personal and professional life.

In her life journey, it emerges clearly that for Emelia, it was never meant to be smooth sailing. She learnt that from a very young age from her family elders, the African way. In her case, it was from her mother, grandmother and countless aunts who helped to ground her in the values and ethics of hard work, honesty, resilience and facing every adversity with hope and confidence.

It was this spirit that lifted her up and kept her going on Jubilee Hill with an indifferent father; after Wesley Girls High School when she failed to get into medical school; facing racism in America when with a Ph.D. she could not find a job commensurate with her rich credentials or even back home in Ghana, failing to be integrated into "the system" after returning from the diaspora very highly qualified, with rich and diversified experiences and determined to contribute one's quota to nation building. Not to mention the challenges of living the "nomadic life" of an international public servant, especially a mother raising children at the same time.

In the end, it is a truly inspiring book. A story of a humble Ghanaian-American, which contains many lessons for each and every one of us.

I wish you a pleasant reading.

Mohamed Ibn Chambas,
Former President of ECOWAS Commission and Former
United Nations Undersecretary-General. African Union
Representative for Silencing the Guns in Africa
Accra, Ghana

CHAPTER 1

Everyone has a story to tell. These stories are filled with love, hope, challenges, opportunities, and regrets. My story starts when I'm a little girl, maybe two or three or four years old, growing up in a suburb of Kumasi in the Ashanti region of Ghana. With a population of 108,000, Kumasi in 1951 was a relatively small city although it was the second largest city in the country besides Accra, the capital. Almost everyone knew everyone else, and communities were formed based on churches attended. Being a vibrant commercial center in the center of the country, it was inhabited by different groups of people from other regions, cities, and villages who were looking for new opportunities and growth. A number of suburbs were named after the predominant groups living there. We had an Ashanti New Town with a predominantly Ashanti population and Fanti New Town where migrating Fantis from the coastal regions congregated. Zongo had the Hausas, Dagombas, and Fulanis from the northern regions.

I do not remember all the details, but I know while growing up in Suame, then a small suburb of Kumasi, I was happy and had a good childhood surrounded by numerous family and family friends. Our home was constantly full of people and activities. My mom, Agnes Turkson, was a certified midwife with her own private practice on the ground floor of Papa Kofi Ntia's house.

When I was two or three years old, we lived in a two-bedroom apartment on the top floor of the house. At the time, it was the only building with more than one story in Old Suame, on the main road from Kumasi to Tamale. This was a major North-South road, a busy thoroughfare filled with timber trucks carrying three heavy logs each from the interior of the forests in the Ashanti region on their way to the only national harbor at the time, in Takoradi, for export.

There were always numerous small passenger trucks plying the Tamale route, laden with loads of personal goods and merchandise purchased by traders and travelers from Kumasi to the shops in the northern part of the country. With the narrow thoroughfare, a single lane in each direction, one had to be careful crossing the road. The noise was overpowering, with cars swerving and horns blowing constantly to alert other drivers and pedestrians to move out of the way. The air was constantly filled with the rich brown dust from vehicles that sometimes drove on the untarred sections of the road to avoid the potholes. In the midst of all this were pedestrians moving-briskly to work, running errands, and the endless stream of sellers balancing their goods on the trays they carried on their heads, running to and from car to car, selling as much as quickly as they could. Thus, everyone appreciated the calm of the evening when the traffic slowed to a normal pace.

Papa Kofi Ntia's house was home. This building housed at least fifteen different families. On the top floor next to our apartment was Maame Ekua with her husband and son, Brobbey, originally from Offinso, thirty miles from Kumasi. Also upstairs was Papa

*Emelia at about
one year old*

Tuffour and his wife, Maame Adwoa Ago. Papa Tuffour was a driver plying passengers from Kumasi to Offinso. He would often come home totally drunk, and we would hear the screams coming from his room as he fought with his wife. We wondered what was happening and often sneaked by the adults to hear their conversations about the constant quarrels emanating from Papa Tuffour's drinking. Apau from Kyekyewere lived alone so his drinking did not cause any havoc for the people in the house.

Right at the entrance to the house on the lower floor was Papa Ensunyameye (his name means "there is nothing God cannot do") and his family. His wife, Maame Serwah, was one of the favorites in the house. She owned a chop bar (a local restaurant) just outside of the house. It was always teeming with customers coming to buy her delicious peanut butter soup and *abitee*, a carbohydrate dish made from dried cassava and molded into large round balls surrounded with soup. We could not escape the awesome aroma of the hot pepper and ginger seasoned peanuts emanating from the small unfinished shed of a chop bar filling the entire house. She would often send some of us children to the nearby market for one type of produce or the other and would always ensure she left some soup for us to enjoy as a treat.

The story goes that originally the Suame house belonged to Papa Ensunyameye. Due to financial problems with the family's cocoa farm in Offinso, he had to sell the house and rent a unit for himself and his family. The financial responsibilities fell on his wife who worked day and night to support the family.

Emelia's mother,
Agnes Turkson, in Suame

Also living in the house were Maame Akosua and her family. Maame Akosua's two daughters, Nana Yaa and Afia Sarpong, were my playmates. Nana Yaa was my age. We both attended Practice School together and would always walk together in the morning to New Suame to fetch buckets of water for our baths before leaving for school. Nana Yaa and I would fetch our water from the nearby township public tap, about three hundred yards from the house. We would stop and play with our neighborhood friends along the way. With all the playing and splashing, we would always come back with our buckets only half full. For us children, getting a bucket of water and gathering together outside at dawn or dusk to bathe was the norm, and it was a lot of fun. We would share jokes and gossip both from school and at home and entertain ourselves. For those with small buckets of water, the challenge was to ensure it was enough to wash away all the soap suds we loved to create.

Maame French, a tenant, got her name due to her trading between Kumasi and francophone Abidjan on Ivory Coast, now Cote d'Ivoire. She would spend weeks buying materials and other supplies from the main Kejetia market, packing and organizing them into bales and carting them off in the middle of the night to Abidjan to sell. On her return she would bring perfumes, jewelry, and ready-made clothes to sell to her numerous local customers in Kumasi. There were never enough for her customers so she ensured she made the trip at least once a month. For us children in the house, the packages of foreign biscuits she would bring back were something we looked forward to. We would make sure we were close by her door when she came home from her errands in town so she could not possibly forget about us when she traveled.

Another tenant Maa had a particular fondness for was Maame Kyekye from Komenda in the Central region, along the main road between Cape Coast and Takoradi. She lived in one of the downstairs rooms with her two daughters, Olofro and Odofroko. The two made an interesting pair. Olofro, the older one, was quiet and submissive to a fault and always stayed close to home. The younger, Odofroko, was extremely hardworking and a different tale from her sister. She used to get up at dawn to be one of the first traders to arrive at the Ayigya market on the other end of town, on the Accra Road, to sell pigs' feet at her popular stand.

One evening I was awakened suddenly by a lot of noise coming from downstairs. I woke up groggily but soon jumped up when I heard a lot of commotion. What could be happening so late in the evening? In the midst of the commotion, Maame Kyekye was wailing inconsolably in the open courtyard of the house. What could be going on?

"Odofroko is gone with that murderer—what will become of her?" Maame Kyekye cried. Doors were pulled open, and sleeping couples rushed out with their clothes tied just above their chests. Everyone ran from their rooms to find out what had happened. Of course, children were not allowed to hear the details, but looking through the throng of women around Maame Kyekye, we overheard her telling the adults of the sudden disappearance of Odofroko.

"My daughter is gone, why is this happening to me after all my struggles?" Maame Kyekye kept asking. She had heard from her fellow market sellers that the girl had run away with a man whose girlfriend had been killed by armed robbers under mysterious circumstances. Clearly, there was some intrigue going on which we did not fully comprehend but we knew something major had happened to her daughter. We all surmised that having made a bit of money from her market sales, she had decided to move out of her mother's reach and discipline.

The Suame house was never a dull place. Papa Akowia from the Brong Ahafo region was a driver plying a passenger transport bus to several destinations in the country. His two wives stayed in separate homes not far from our house. He never failed, though, to bring home one concubine after another from each of his distant travels. One of these concubines, a Krobo woman Maame Akosua from Somanya in the Eastern region, eventually became his third and favorite wife. She was a beautiful woman, always with her hair impeccably styled and fashionably dressed, and we overheard grownups talking about the beauty of the women from the Krobo area. She was always impeccably dressed, and we would stare at her in awe of how pretty

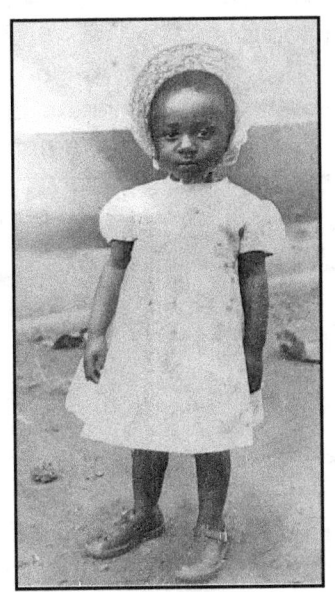

Emelia at about age three

she looked. She settled in and set up a provisions shop outside the house. Her shop was always full, some just coming through to admire her beauty. The room under the stairs was for Maame Adwoa Gyaama and her mother who had a stall at the Kejetia market selling saucepans.

There were others who lived in this house, too, with only one bathroom and a toilet upstairs and another set downstairs. I never heard of any quarrels or saw any queues behind the toilet or bathroom. There was a public toilet not far from the house, and we would always run in that direction when we had to.

***

The Shell gas station across the street from our house was the center of evening activities. It was the main station for the Suame bread sellers grouped together and gossiping about the neighborhood's affairs, their loaves of bread sitting in pans supported on their heads. To see them stop mid-sentence and quickly jump up to run to any vehicle that pulled into the gas station to sell their loaves without ever disturbing the bundles on their heads was a sight to behold.

wAt the time not many homes had electricity so the lights at the gas station were a magnet in the evenings. Neighborhood youth would congregate around the *kelewele* (fried plantain spiced with

Maame Yaa in Suame about 2000

ginger, hot pepper, and onions) sellers, and old men would sit under the nearby trees smoking their pipes, sipping their Club or Star branded beers, and enjoying the evening cooler weather.

By night it was the Shell station for the community, and by day it was Mr. Forduor's shop. It was the main shop in Suame for fabrics, electrical wares, and most household needs. Being right on the main road, everyone passing would stop by to greet Mr. Forduor. He was one of the most affluent people in the town, besides the three Gyamfi brothers, and was highly respected. His shop therefore was a center of social life and gathering.

***

Growing up I knew I had two moms. The house next to our building was owned by Papa Kwesi Darkwa, then the secretary of the Asantehene, the eminent ruler of the Ashanti Kingdom, Otumfuor Nana Osei Tutu Agyeman Prempeh II. With his position in the Manhyia palace, Papa Darkwa was a renowned member of society and was held in very high esteem. His first wife, Maame Yaa Mabre, had no children, and she was Maa's best friend. He had eight children by his second wife, and most of them lived in the house. The older ones, sister Baby and Joe, were married and lived with their families. The younger ones still in school stayed with Maame Yaa and their dad. Unlike our house, all the people in Mr. Darkwa's house were relatives—children or cousins.

Maame Yaa's stepchildren were not always pleasant to her. She would often come crying to Maa to tell her one story or another about the stepchildren and to complain about her husband not standing by her when the children misbehaved. She would spend a lot of time with Maa and, in the process, took a particular interest in me. She had her own stall at the Kejetia market and would go each day to sell her wares. Her stall was filled wall to wall with traditional Dutch wax print fabrics and scarves imported from Holland for sale.

While Maa was busy with her maternity home, Maame Yaa took me under her wing as if I was her own. Off I went to the market with her and would stay all day until we returned in the evening. I loved being in the market, playing with other children who had come with their parents. The Kejetia market has traditionally been the largest outdoor market in Ghana, and we used to claim, "even West Africa!" The market bustled with people pushing and shoving through the crowds. From the carpark to the stalls, the numerous pushcarts conveying all types of merchandise fanned out in all directions and took up a lot of space. It took forever to move through them to where you needed to go. Everywhere you turned, people were screaming at the owners and their pushcarts to get out of the way. The noise was always deafening.

Maame Yaa's stall was past the stench of the section with the butchers and the fowl sellers. You would have to hold your breath and move as fast as you could to get through that section. As is true in markets throughout that part of the world, stalls were arranged in sections selling the same items or in the same category. Thus, whether you were in the market to buy vegetables, meat, cleaning supplies, or building supplies, you knew where to go and could plan your day and would readily find the particular section of the market, thus shopping with utmost efficiency.

Each group of traders organized themselves into associations to support each other. They knew each other's families and issues of concern. The fellow traders realized how special I had made life for

Maame Yaa, and I was completely accepted by all of them and pampered with all I needed. I remember my daily lunch of roasted ripe plantain and peanuts, sometimes *ofam* (baked pounded plantain seasoned with hot pepper and ginger). Lunch was always followed by my nap. Maame Yaa's friends would shower me with presents, put me on their laps, and sing for me. They would braid and re-braid my hair and ensure I had plenty of toys to occupy me while I was in the market. If anyone was going shopping or running an errand in other parts of the market, they would take me along. I had a wonderful time with all the women making me feel very special, and also important. We would generally leave the market early by 3:30 p.m. to get home, have a bath, and then eat the evening meal of *fufu* (pounded green plantain and cassava) and soup. On weekdays it would be light vegetable soup, with the palm nut soup and peanut butter soup reserved for Saturdays and Sundays.

***

A day came when my mom said I would no longer go to the market with Maame Yaa. I had to start kindergarten at the Practice School down the road, by the main Suame roundabout. The school was a fifteen-minute walk from the house at the intersection with the Suame Police Station and the Water and Sewerage Company. I dreaded parting with Maame Yaa and insisted I did not need to go to any school. I cried for days, and my mom kept assuring me that I would enjoy it once I started. I did not believe her. How was I going to spend the day without my Maame Yaa? For the first time my fussing was not enough for my mom to relent and give up.

The eventful first day of school arrived, and Maa dressed me, cheering me up each step of the way. I was not happy with my new yellow and green uniform. I was not happy with my brand-new brown Bata Clarks walking shoes and dainty white socks. Maa thought I would be happy since I had seen other schoolchildren wearing those same leather shoes with sturdy soles and straps across the front of the feet. I had yearned for them. The fact that they had come from overseas made them so special. Now I had them and was still fussing. I cried all the way to school. The first week of school was both fun and miserable. I had a lot of fun with my newfound friends outside of the Kejetia market yet missed the play time at the market. Maame Yaa did not go to the market for the first two weeks I was in school, worried I might get hurt outside her watchful eyes.

Thus, the first two weeks I would get home from school and go straight to Maame Yaa's house where she was waiting for me. I would jump into her warm embrace and fill her in on how my day had been. I would generally spend the rest of the afternoon with her, joining her in having her regular evening meal of *fufu* and whatever version of light soup had been prepared before going home to my mom's house. In an Ashanti home, you would not have eaten dinner unless you had *fufu* so I was guaranteed my own big bowl of *fufu* with her every evening. The light soup can sometimes be made with *prekese* (a flowering plant said to have excellent medicinal properties) or with green vegetables to make *ebunebunu (green leaf soup)* and a whole range of other variations to give some variety. The *fufu* normally is made with green plantain and cassava, cooked and pounded into a pulp. When in season, it can be made from yams or from cocoyam. This ensured there was variety in both the type of *fufu* as well as the soup. Even then I marveled at the fact that we would eat *fufu* each and every day. I yearned for variety so I would eat the *fufu* in Maame Yaa's house and then go home to eat rice or whatever else Maa had cooked. We did not eat *fufu* in my mother's house; you would only see it prepared when we had guests who wanted it. As a Fanti, *kenkey* (fermented corn, partially cooked, and then wrapped with plantain leaves and boiled till fully cooked) was our staple with stew, fish, or meat and was more a regular dish as well as several variations of rice and *ampesi* (boiled tubers, plantain, cocoyam).

Kumasi is in the center of the forest region of Ghana, with heavy annual rainfall during the long rainy seasons. It is known as the Garden City due to the lushness of the plant life and the numerous gardens and parks in most communities. Most houses, gardens, and compounds are planted with evergreen trees such as the green-leaved neem trees and the Flamboyant trees with their broad spreading, umbrella-like canopies and their beautiful orange flowers. In the afternoon the men would sit under the Flamboyant's shade playing board games. Others had fruit trees including mango, almond, and papaya. In the more affluent areas of the city where the compounds were much larger, beautiful flower beds burst with the color of lovely bougainvillea and hibiscus hedges along the walls surrounding the massive homes.

As children we loved to take the short walk to the Odeon Cinema on weekends to watch Indian and Zorro films, or just idly walk around the nearby racecourse with friends to while away time. On Sundays we would dress up in our frilly outfits and get in a taxi for services at the Central Methodist Church, in Adum, in the center of Kumasi, next to the prison. We always wondered why there would be a prison next to the church, but it was not for us to discern, only to note and marvel. We knew the church well since it was also the same church that all *Mmofraturo* students attended the Sunday after each annual Speech Day celebrations. The enormous pipe organ with its deep resounding tone provided an entirely different sound to the hymns we all knew and memorized regularly at school. We grew up as happy children, feeling extremely secure, loved, and admired by family, friends, and the community at large. We were blessed with an inner sense of peace and contentment.

CHAPTER 2

That way of life was not to last forever. It must have been at the end of the first term when I was in Class 2 (second grade equivalent) when my mom told me I was going away to a different school, in Elmina, for Class 3. I had no idea about the school, or Elmina for that matter, but I knew I did not want to leave Kumasi and Maame Yaa and go anywhere. I threw a lot of tantrums during the ensuing days and weeks. "Please let me stay! I'll be good. I'll do my homework. Please." Maa, as far as I could see, was paying little attention to my tantrums.

I was happy, though, to go shopping with her over the weekends when she was not working, to shop for me to go to this new school. She told me she had a prospectus with the list of items I needed to take to school. Generally, when Maa bought anything for me, she also bought something similar for my cousins who were staying with us and for my brothers as well. Suddenly, she was buying things only for me, which made me feel very special.

Emelia kneeling in front with Maa and friends at the Methodist Conference, Kumasi, 1961

I had my own trunk, a large metal box with a hinged lid for storage, which she took to a special place so they could emboss my name on it. She had the carpenter next door make my own special chop box for me. The chop box is a large wooden box that students kept their provisions in. I was learning about all this as the days went by. Before long, I had a trunk with new Ghana cloth for church services and special occasions, dresses for daily wear, and new school uniforms with colors different from the ones I wore at Practice School.

By the end of the school year my chop box was loaded with *gari* (grated and dried roasted cassava), Titus brand sardines from Portugal, boxes of Cabin biscuits and cream crackers in the traditional blue and white box, cans of Heinz baked beans, and two big bottles of *shittor*, spiced pepper and shrimp sauce, specially prepared for me by Sister Ama Benewah, Maa's help, who had been sent to stay with her shortly after moving to Suame to start her midwifery practice. The *shittor* was cooked for a long time, until it eventually attained a dark brown color effused with bits of onions, dried shrimp and fish, and cayenne pepper. It was the perfect condiment to have with gari and sardines. Since it will not spoil outside the refrigerator, it was the perfect condiment to take to a boarding school away from home.

Elmina is a small town in the Central region of Ghana on the Gulf of Guinea. It is primarily a fishing town renowned for two main national institutions. Elmina was one of the key centers of the slave trade along the Gulf Coast of West Africa and has the oldest castle in sub-Saharan Africa. The Elmina Castle, now a UNESCO World Heritage Site and a major tourist attraction, was built by the Portuguese in 1482 as Castelo de Sao Jorge da Mina (St. George of the Mine Castle).

The castle, first established as a trade settlement, later became one of the most important stops on the route of the trans-Atlantic slave trade. The Dutch seized the fort from the Portuguese in 1637 and continued with the slave trade from there until 1814. The castle's strategic position on the beach with rows of enormous coconut trees swaying in its shadows has been central to Ghana's global history. The broad swath of green surrounding it served as a place for community gatherings and sporting activities.

Elmina is also renowned for one of the national annual festivals. *Bakatue,* literally meaning the "draining of the lagoon," is an important festival for the fishing town and celebrated each July by the chiefs and people of Elmina. It marks the beginning of the fishing season and to give thanks and prayers to the local gods to ensure they have a fruitful harvest of fish. It is the annual major occasion for local chiefs in the traditional areas to don their colorful kente cloths and be paraded through the streets in their palanquins. The *bakatue* durbars attract people from all around the country to see the durbar and the flotilla of boats on the lagoon filled with men fishing heartily and to return any catch for the day back to the waters as a dedication to the sea god.

***

My new school, Our Lady of Apostles (OLA) perched on top of the hill in Elmina, was a Catholic boarding school, although there were day students who attended from Elmina and some of the neighboring communities. OLA was part of a network of OLA schools across the country, primarily for girls. It had a very large compound with four large dormitories on the hilltop next to the Roman Catholic Church and its ancient Dutch cemetery.

The main buildings were composed of a network of dormitories, classrooms, and an assembly hall enclosing a huge compound. The layout enabled one to see what was happening on the interior compound no matter where you were. The school had students in the primary grades from Class 1 to Class 6 and middle school from Form 1 to Form 4. Students were sent from across the country—some on scholarship, others paying full fees—from all economic and social classes. Mother Ursula, our Headmistress, was a stern disciplinarian, and we all feared her. The other sisters, led by Sister Stanislaus, however, were loving, kind women who cared for us and tolerated all our whims with love and patience.

Initially, it was difficult to adjust. I was so young, and Elmina was very far from Kumasi. My mom had some friends living in Elmina to whom she made sure that I was introduced and who became my guardians. Additionally, there were other older students from Kumasi whose families my mom knew who were asked to look out for me and take care of me.

On most weekends, my guardian would bring me food and always included my favorite *polo* biscuit, which was a biscuit made with grated coconut, well-seasoned with nutmeg and cinnamon, rolled and baked to a crispy flake. I waited anxiously each weekend for my *polo* and sometimes would even give money to the day students to buy some for me from town. The coastlines were lined with numerous rows of coconut trees, and it became a tradition in Elmina to make the *polo* and sell it all over the country.

There were so many memorable occasions at OLA. Not long after Independence on 6 March 1957, we were informed the Queen of England was to visit Elmina and all students were to attend a welcome parade for her. "Who is the Queen? Is she an *obroni,* meaning a white person, coming from overseas? What has she got to do with our Independence?" "Do we get to shake hands with her?" "Perhaps the school photographer can take photos of us with the Queen." The questions kept coming from all of us to the teachers. When we understood the importance and significance of the visit, we could not wait to be a part of it. The excitement in the whole country, and for us in Elmina, grew. This was a once in a lifetime event and a not-to-be-missed occasion.

Preparations were made in earnest at school and elsewhere in the town with the red, yellow, and green flags of the newly Independent Ghana hanging on all the light posts. Wherever they could afford the luxury, houses began to shine bright with a new coat of paint. After weeks of practicing our songs and marching drills we were ready when the day finally arrived. There was a lot of anticipation. We had waited so long for this day. We barely slept the night before the event, chatting and giggling at the possibility of meeting a Queen from abroad. We woke up early before we even heard the usual wake-up bell ringing. Uniforms had been well starched and ironed ahead of time, and our Clarks sandals were polished to a shine. We needed no encouragement to get ready and get to assembly for our march down the hill into town. The usual dragging of feet to make the long walk to town for other occasions turned into brisk enthusiastic strides for the much-anticipated event.

We lined up in front of the main post office with our sweat going unnoticed under the midday sun. We must have waited forever but eventually our voices screamed with excitement, waving the small national flags we each held, as the Queen's motorcade passed on the way to the Elmina Castle and onwards to the chief's palace to meet with the dignitaries gathered there. We were later each given a mug with the Queen's image and royal emblem to serve as a souvenir for the occasion.

***

The long stretch of land in front of the Elmina Castle was one of my favorite places. All our main athletic events with other OLA schools took place at the track in front of the castle. The numerous rows of coconut trees along the beach provided much needed shade, and the ocean breezes were always welcome. At the beach, we were sure that Beatrice Ngizza, the small lanky student from my dormitory who always won the 100-meter dash race, was really not a fast runner but rather was swept to victory by the breeze.

We looked forward to the sports days and the competition. All the schools with their different sports colors—blues and greens and reds and yellows—would be seen gathering in different sections of the stretch of the park. The 4x110 yards and the 4x220 yards relays were always the best. Everyone would jump up and down with excitement as their teams moved by screaming and cheering their teams on, stopping occasionally to sip coconut juice, as needed. It was always so hot and humid but we didn't mind. We would make sure to buy some coconuts from the market women who would set up on the beach to join in the fun and make some money as well.

Elmina was always known as a city full of evil spirits and witches. Our school compound was next to the Roman Catholic Church, and directly behind it was the Catholic cemetery, previously the Dutch cemetery. Down in the valley from the top of the hill where our school was situated was the stream and lagoon, which emptied further down into the Atlantic Ocean. The section of the stream below us was the main site for the annual main festival in Elmina to inaugurate the fishing season, *Bakatue*.

We were always scared of ghosts and witches. The dormitory rooms could sleep at least thirty students in the junior grades with beds in three rows across the room, one row lined up against the long row of windows closest to the outside veranda. The second row was against the wall closest to the cemetery, and there was a middle row, which was where my bed was. At night we would put all the beds together in the middle row so we felt secure and not alone.

One fateful night, a number of us woke after midnight to see three glowing balls of bright yellow surrounded by red light shining into the dormitory from the outside veranda. Our terrified screams filled the air, waking up the entire school. Those lights confirmed what we had always been told that the compound was haunted and the witches and ghosts of Elmina roamed freely at night everywhere. We never slept on the middle beds again. We always joined our friends closest to the veranda with our heads facing the main wall so we could no longer see anything from the outside at night. Part of me still carries that mystery of the lights of Elmina. Whether they were truly witches and ghosts, children's wild imagination, or perhaps the lights from the nuns' flashlights as they went on their nightly inspections was never resolved.

From these early years at the boarding school, the importance of school achievement was drilled into all of us. Most of the teachers were white nuns with a few Ghanaians among them. All the teachers recognized the different potential in each student and would always dedicate extra time with individual students to ensure everyone was doing well. There were a number of students from prominent political or wealthy families. There was absolutely no distinction in the treatment and support provided to the students. The one thing that stood out was the ability of the wealthy families to organize school wide birthday parties with *fufu* and peanut soup and *jollof* rice with lots of chicken and drinks. No one really knew their families had money until we had those birthday parties. Apart from the food, the wealth meant very little to most students. For us, it was a real treat and fun times on those occasions.

CHAPTER 3

At about the age of ten, I was moved from OLA Girls School at Elmina to another girls boarding school in Kumasi called *Mmofraturo,* a Methodist Girls Boarding School founded in 1930. *Mmofraturo* was a Middle School for Forms 1 to 4, after which you received the Middle School Leaving Certificate, equivalent to a high school diploma in the United States. It was steeped in the Methodist tradition and supported financially by the Methodist Church of Ghana. There was a great linkage with the pastors and elders of the Kumasi Methodist Circuit who would come to preach at the Sunday services at the school.

I was too young to appreciate the joys of boarding school at the OLA Girls School in Elmina. For that reason, Maa had decided I needed to be reintroduced to the family's Methodist tradition. I remember my mom remarking that the Catholic daily masses we were attending at OLA were causing my knees to darken more than usual. Only in a child's mind will something like that register for so long. Whatever her reason for moving me, I was just happy to be back in Kumasi and closer to home. Although it was again an all-girls boarding school, it was within walking distance from home, barely a twenty-minute walk, so whenever the opportunity for an exeat was provided, I hurried on home with friends for Mom's food and lingered till it was absolutely time to run back to school.

Mmofraturo literally means "children's garden," and it turned out to be exactly what the name implied. Around the time I transferred to *Mmofraturo,* Maame Yaa and her husband, Papa Darkwa, built a new house across the street from the school gate. It was a blessed time for me, full of friends at school and family very close by. I was a very happy student.

For some reason, I was selected with another classmate, Elizabeth Yaa Agyeiwaa Mensah—affectionately called by her middle initials Y.A.—to be the house help for the senior prefect, Sister Mercy Agyen. We were to run her errands and provide any support she needed. Sister Mercy loved the slightly burnt bottom of the rice, which was not served to us in the dining hall. The school cooks would give that to whoever wanted it; this was a real delicacy for most students so there was a lot of competition. We had to make sure to line our bowls in front of the kitchen, and those whose bowls were out first were always assured of getting some "rice under" as we called it.

It was an assignment we took seriously to make sure her bowl was always close to the front of the line. We knew we would benefit from it as well. She would also send us just outside the school gate to buy roasted plantains and peanuts for her. We always felt so big and important because most of our classmates could not venture out of the gate without being punished. We were Sister Mercy's girls,

Kumasi, 1973, with friends: (from left) Yaa, Emelia, Bea, and Afia

which the security at the gate and everyone knew. We both also worked very hard at school with our studies, not wanting to displease Sister Mercy who looked out for us and helped us with our homework and studies. We were also very naughty at times, always chatting and giggling about so many silly things. We were seldom punished, though, because we were the "children" of the senior prefect!

There was a lot of growing up and learning in *Mmofraturo* especially about the Methodist traditions of singing hymns and service to the community. There were monthly singing competitions among the different dormitories to find out which group had best memorized the hymns. It was a lot of fun. We sang everywhere, sitting on stairs in front of the dorms, on the way to the school garden, and in the bathrooms. Saturday mornings were devoted to voluntary work in the neighboring communities of Kurofrom or Tafo sweeping and collecting garbage from along the streets to ensure cleanliness. Gardens around the dormitories were tended by those of us in the junior year, with the seniors supervising and sitting and chatting. We always thought it was not fair.

One thing we dreaded the most was Ms. Offei's math class. She would always start with mental examinations. She expected us to have memorized the multiplication table and quizzed us on the table. If you were unable to give the answer in a second, you were in trouble. She put two rulers together, asked you to put your fingers together and raise your hand up, then she beat you on the clasped fingers a couple of times with the rulers. That was torture. One of those beatings and you never needed a reminder that it was important to focus during studies and memorize the multiplication table.

My time at *Mmofraturo* went by so quickly. Before I realized it, two years had passed and it was time for the secondary school Common Entrance examinations. Mostly an aptitude test in English and Mathematics, it was not an easy exam. If you received a passing grade in Forms 2, 3, or 4, you were sent to a secondary school. Almost all the students longed to pass and gain entrance into the country's premier girls' secondary school, Wesley Girls High School located in Kakumdu, a suburb of Cape Coast in the Central Region.

I took the exam in Form 2. The day the results came in, the headmistress, Ms. Beatrice Owusu-Afram, a heavy-set, caring, and affectionate lady, stood on the first-floor balcony of the Administration Building. All the expectant students were standing downstairs and looking up to her, praying for their names to be called as having passed. If they did, they would be admitted to Wesley Girls and other secondary schools across the country. I don't even recall hearing my name in all the excitement. All I remember was being pushed by some of my friends and running up those winding stairs to collect my admission letter from Wesley Girls. Yes,

I got in, and the smiles and laughter of all my other friends who got admission swirled around us for the rest of the semester.

After reading the list, Ms. Owusu-Afram shook her heavy-set arms and said, "Here you are, and there you are." For those who did not get the admission for the current year, it was a period of unbearable pain and misery with the headmistress's words perceived as adding salt to the injury. One could then only wait and hope for better results in the subsequent years.

In all the celebrations, though, I felt a pinch of sadness knowing that Y.A. and I were going to be separated after our wonderful time together. I was going to Wesley Girls, an all-girls secondary school in Cape Coast, but she was going to Achimota School in Accra. Achimota was founded in 1924 by Sir Frederick Guggisburg, a British Governor of the Gold Coast; Dr. James Kwegyir Aggrey, a Ghanaian intellectual; and the Rev. Alec Gordon Fraser, a British Anglican vicar. Achimota was modeled on the British public school system. It was the first mixed-gender school to be established in the Gold Coast. Since our families live in Kumasi, not far from each other, we promised we would spend time together during the summer break and school holidays.

In my mind the time spent at *Mmofraturo* comes back to me in fits and starts. There are aspects I remember in detail. However, Y.A. remembers all the details. To this day, each time we talk to each other she reminds me of all the naughty things we used to do together. The stories never end.

CHAPTER 4

For my three brothers and me, our lives revolved around Maa and her side of the family. Her two sisters, Auntie Mamaa (Letitia Turkson) and Auntie Virg (Virginia Turkson), lived in Kumasi. Auntie Mamaa for a while lived in the same yellow house where I was born until she moved to Kejetia to stay in the family house where my grandma, Maame Amma Atta (Grace Fynn), lived with a range of other relatives. Auntie Mamaa had a stall at the main Kumasi Kejetia market where she sold household goods such as pots and pans. Staying at Kejetia allowed her to walk to the market instead of struggling to go to work in the public *trotro* buses. Her two older children, Cynthia and Rosebay Halm, were grown up and worked in Accra. Her four younger children, Minnette, Maudlin, Kojo, and Marjorie Halm, all lived with me, my siblings, and my mom in our Suame house. Minnette and I were soon going to be together at Wesley Girls High School as well.

My Auntie Virg lived in her small estate house at South Suntresu near the main Okomfo Anokye Hospital where she worked as one of the matrons in the Nurses Training College. Her husband, Mr. Essandoh, worked at the Kumasi City Council in the accounts section. Three of her children, Edith, Kofi, and Atom, stayed with them in Suntreso. Two other daughters, Regina and Ophelia Essandoh, lived with us in Suame. One was surrounded and emotionally supported not only by close family members but by an entire community who looked out for the welfare of all the children, as was common in our traditional African culture.

We had a full and bustling house in Suame. By the time I started *Mmofraturo* my mom had completed the building of her own house just across the street from our old multi-family yellow house on the busy Kumasi Tamale Road. It was a grand two-story building with a large compound and a balcony upstairs overlooking the shops in the valley below us. Behind our house was a heavily forested area with distant views of the Tafo main cemetery. Next to it was the Suame Methodist Church. Our new home was the center of all family activities. My mom was doing well financially with her bustling and busy maternity home and her bread business. Turkson's maternity home was one of a handful of private midwifery centers in Kumasi serving the city as well as neighboring towns and villages. At the time there was a maximum of ten private midwives throughout the city to service that large population, and most patients preferred going to the midwives instead of the main hospital.

Emelia's home and her mother's clinic in Suame

All the private midwives at the time had been trained either at the national flagship hospital in Accra, Korle Bu, and were competent professionals that patients could depend on. They were all affiliated with the Central Okomfo Anokye Hospital in Kumasi and could readily refer patients there in case of emergency. The warm and pleasant atmosphere in these maternity homes and the dedicated care by the midwives and their assistants attracted patients from all the neighboring towns and villages, which relieved pressure as well on the main hospital.

At the time the population of the Kumasi metropolitan area was about 200,000 people. Maa's clinic was affiliated and accredited by the Ministry of Health, and we always had, at any one time, two training midwives from the Okomfo Anokye Nurses and Midwifery Training School on three months' full-time assignments in our home. This secondment, or temporary transfer, of the students provided them with hands-on experience as part of their training. It was a very busy practice with patients coming in from as far out as Offinso, thirty miles from Suame. On Tuesday mornings, when they organize the well-baby clinics with support from the Okomfo Anokye Children's Center, our home would be full all day with mothers and their babies. Mothers came from the villages with presents from their farms for Mom and the other midwives, especially during the harvest seasons. We always had regular supplies of bananas, mangoes, plantains, yams, and vegetables from the farmers' wives.

The midwifery was on the top floor of the house. Our living quarters—consisting of three bedrooms, a living and dining room, a kitchen, and a bath and toilet—were on the lower floor. The middle bedroom, where the girls slept, was directly below the Labor Ward; growing up hearing the cries of women in labor was a very frequent occurrence. We always heard them at night crying, screaming they would never have another child, only to see them in the morning in the Lying-in ward with smiles, tenderly holding their babies. Many of these women were back in two years or so for the delivery of the next baby. Many families in the area had up to six or seven children all birthed in Maa's maternity. Turkson's Maternity became home to a lot of families.

In addition to the resident midwives from the Okomfo Anokye Hospital, there were permanent midwives who worked for Maa and lived in the extra rooms upstairs with their families. Auntie Martha and Sister Elizabeth were two of those who stayed the longest with us. There was also Grace, a midwifery assistant. Auntie Martha was a tall, very dark-skinned woman from the Brong Ahafo region. She lived with her sister Yaa who was my age and my best friend in the house. Auntie Martha loved to play the lotteries. The Ghana Lotteries at the time had become very popular with everyone seeking to get rich quickly. Out of that evolved Lotto "Doctors" who swore they could calculate the seven numbers to be drawn for the Saturday evening lottery draw. It was a lot of fun to spend time on the upstairs balcony when there were no patients to be cared for by Auntie Martha and her Lotto Doctors. They would spend hours computing numbers each day and would swear they had the definite numbers for the week only to be disappointed when the numbers came out.

Sometimes Auntie Martha would win up to fifty Ghana cedis for getting four to five numbers correct in the drawing. That always called for a celebration. With her winnings collected on Sunday she would always prepare her favorite meal: peanut butter soup and *kokonte* or *lapiiwa*. *Kokonte,* which is a *fufu*-like mash made from dried and grated cassava and a very popular dish for the people from the northern part of Ghana. That was then. Now it has become one of the major staples throughout the country for both the rich and the poor alike. For most catered events including funerals, engagements, and family parties, people will now always request the hosts to include *Kokonte* on the menu.

Auntie Martha had one third of her teeth gone, and the remaining were spread unevenly in her mouth. We would tease her as children, and she would get so mad at us. She would tell us not to come close again when she and her gurus were working on the Lotto numbers. But we always did. She would soon forget and call us to come hang out with her or to send us across the street to the Nigerian ladies' shop to buy her one thing or the other.

There was also the year we had Mister Donkor staying in one of the rooms in our upstairs extension to our home. You never knew when Maa would bring someone to the house in need of temporary accommodation or food. Mr. Donkor had just moved to Kumasi to start a church ministry. He had negotiated with the Methodist Church next door to use their premises for his evening church meetings. He was an affable man of about forty years old with a very contagious laugh and full of jokes. It did not take him much time to suddenly grow the small congregation he had started. Each Friday evening the congregation would go to Breman, a hillside suburb, for an all-night service in the mountains just outside Kumasi.

In the afternoons when Mr. Donkor had no prior commitments, he would put a mat on the floor of the upstairs compound, lie on his back with his hands under his head, and sing hymns for hours. This hymn singing was mixed with the traditional melodies and beats we all enjoyed. We would all invariably join in periodically as our day allowed or listen to him as we carried on with our chores. He would gather us around him in the evenings and tell us stories about the proud Ashanti Kingdom and the various wars they fought to defend their territory. He would tell us stories about the cultures of the different ethnic groups in Ghana and always stressed the importance of learning and ensuring we did well in school.

***

In addition to the midwifery practice, Maa's bakery employed more than eight people and supplied different kinds of bread including the favorite "tea" and "sugar" breads daily to the main department shops in Kumasi, including Kingsway Stores, Glamour, and Ghana National Trading Company (GNTC). The "tea" bread was savory and tasted like Italian bread whereas the "sugar" bread was definitely sweeter, more like Hawaiian bread. The chief bakers were Auntie Ekua and Maame Tawiah. Auntie Ekua had helped another Fanti woman in North Suntresu with her baking business. When the business collapsed, she was referred by one of Maa's Fanti friends. It was timely because Maa was just beginning to organize her baking business. Auntie Ekua came first and would soon be joined by a string of people from her village in Mankessim in the Central Region.

Our home was always bustling with activity, with different people coming to visit, to consult with my mom on issues they were facing in their lives, or to just stop over to buy a loaf of bread and stay on for hours to chitchat with Maa or any of the grownups in and around the house.

As I started developing and maturing over the years, I began to feel alone, despite always being surrounded by so many family members and other relations. My brothers all had their friends they played with outside of school. My cousins would tend to group together and socialize among themselves. There was truly no one close to my age except Ophelia. She had her own circle of friends from the experimental school she attended. I loved to read, and over time I would spend a lot of time alone reading whatever story books we had around the house and asking Maa to buy me new books. I also began to realize that because there were so many young family members in the house who were already attending secondary school, Maa spent a lot of time and money ensuring that everyone was well taken care of and our physical and emotional needs were being met.

One person, though, could not adequately meet all the needs of all of us all the time. I also felt that to ensure that she was not unduly favoring me, her only daughter, over all her nieces and nephews, she would often tell me to be patient and would eventually get for me whatever I needed, which she did. I was slowly learning to be patient and ask for as little as I needed. I was content with whatever I was given, and I did not feel deprived.

At the time I didn't realize that my life was going to be completely turned around with my moving to Wesley Girls High School and Cape Coast.

CHAPTER 5

The summer months of 1964 could not go quickly enough. I was heading to Wesley Girls High School in Kakumdo, Cape Coast. For a young Methodist girl, it was the epitome of success to be able to gain entry into a secondary school from Form 2. In our home that summer, Mom was busy getting me ready. The prospectus was received in June, and we went through the school requirements list expectantly. Several new black and white long skirts and stylish tops were being sewn by Aunty Comfort and Nyaa, the two ladies who sewed any significant piece of outfit for Maa and her friends. Maa ordered a new metal storage box from the carpentry workshop next to our house. On it painted in yellow on the red and black background of the box was my full name: Emelia Ethel Ackah.

The house bustled with excitement. Throughout the summer all the necessary clothes and provisions were slowly being put together. The trip to downtown Kumasi to try on my new Bata sandals, famously called Achimota sandals, happened in August to ensure my fast-growing feet did not outgrow them in the months at home. Sister Ama made sure to make my *shittor* (hot pepper sauce), and, of course, Maame Yaa had to make sure I had one kente cloth made for Speech Day and other important events for which the Kente was needed. The Kente cloth is the traditional handwoven national cloth of Ghana, made of strips of silk and cotton. Kente is more than just a cloth. It is woven to represent Ghanaian history and culture with special designs made to commemorate all special occasions and depicting our history, religious beliefs, and social values.

Maa, always my true cheerleader, told all her friends that I had admission to Wesley Girls, thus every one of them who saw me would congratulate me and encourage me to work as hard as I could when I went there. "Naana, you are going to be a doctor" was their usual refrain. If there was any doubt in my mind that I had to do well, it had completely vanished by the time I set foot at Wesley Girls.

September was a whole new beginning, a new threshold for me. In September, it seems the whole family went with me to Cape Coast. In my entourage was my mom, my two younger brothers,

Nana Apreh and Nana Omiano, as well as Maame Yaa. We all took the Neoplan bus for the one-hundred-and-forty-six-mile, five-hour drive to Cape Coast. The drive took us through the Santasi roundabout on the outskirts of Kumasi, through to Assin Foso, Abura Dunkwa, and on to Yamoransa before joining the main Accra–Cape Coast Road to Abura and then to the main bus stop at Kotokoraba main transport station.

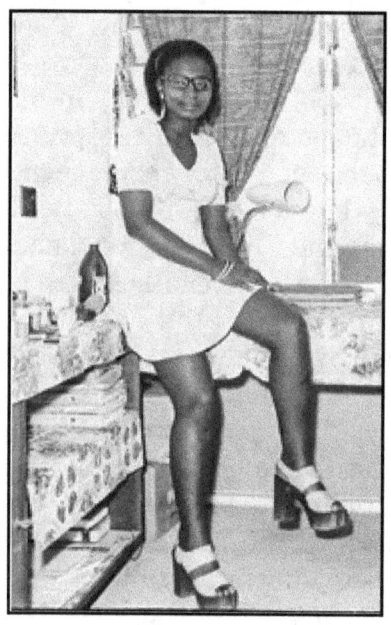

Emelia in her KNUST dorm room, 1974

As we drove toward Cape Coast, we left the forest behind and made our way through the numerous towns and villages, slowly moving into the coastal savanna region along the coast. The public transport buses were always packed with more than thirty passengers from all walks of life. There were traders who had come to buy goods from Kumasi to sell in the villages along the Cape Coast route. The goods were loaded on top of the vehicle and covered with tarpaulin cloth in the event it rained along the way. One would see similar trucks sometimes overloaded with goods and almost ready to topple over along the narrow two-lane road.

Cape Coast is eight miles from Elmina where I had attended primary school. I would have used the same route passing through Cape Coast on my way to Elmina during those days. However, on this trip, I did not quite remember the travels to Elmina each school year. All I remembered was a never-ending long trip on the bus, sleeping most of the way with the lull of the drive. This drive was different. I was older, more aware, and full of excitement for a new beginning.

I memorized the names of the major towns along the route and remembered the rest stop at Fosu and the stop to buy kenkey at Yamoransa Junction. It was a heavily traveled thoroughfare linking the center of the country to the coast and further westward to the harbor city of Takoradi and the national port. On the narrow roads, Timber trucks laden with the usual three heavy logs chained together and heading toward the harbor took control on the narrow roads and slowed traffic considerably. Overtaking them was a challenge for the smaller passenger vehicles already carrying excess weight and unbalanced from the looks of them. It was a long drive, giving me time between my dozing off to dream and wonder what was ahead of me.

I knew I would miss my mom, Maame Yaa, my siblings, and all the cousins who lived with us. I would miss my frequent home trips from school as I had done from *Mmofraturo*. On the positive side, one of my cousins, Minnette, was also attending Wesley Girls. She was two years ahead of me, and I knew she would keep an eye on me. I was happy. She had already told me a lot about the routines at the school and had tried to be patient with me with my incessant questioning throughout the summer. She kept reminding me to hold on to some of my questions and wait so I could be surprised when I got to the school. That was very difficult to do.

Cape Coast was also going to bring a whole new dimension to my life: my father. I had grown up surrounded by so many people who cherished me with love and encouragement. In addition to family members, the entire Suame community at that time constituted a real caring village for all of us children. No matter where you went as a child in the community, all the adults saw you as their responsibility to ensure your welfare, making sure you were behaving properly and not hesitating to reprimand you if you misbehaved or did not speak appropriately. Overall, I felt surrounded with care and love.

CHAPTER 6

Christian Abraham (C.A.) Ackah, my father, lived in his mansion, Baffoa Lodge, named after his mother, with his other family. Until I went to Cape Coast, I can't ever remember asking my mom or anyone else about my father. It was never something I thought about, and I don't recall anyone talking to me about my father. Growing up, children did not ask such questions.

I guess, in retrospect, I had no want of material things since Maa provided abundantly for me and I was surrounded by so many relatives. There were a lot of families with only the mother around so growing up with only your mother wasn't surprising or unusual. My cousins, the Halms, also did not have a father around. I don't recall ever meeting him, though no one said anything about his passing. It was many years later when I heard he lived in Accra with his other wife.

I was entering a whole new phase of life on both the school front and the family front in Cape Coast. When I was getting ready to go to Wesley Girls, my mom informed me that my dad lived in Cape Coast so I would get to meet him. At the time I don't recall this conversation as a major event. There was just so much excitement already about my new school, and all I wanted was to get there.

Still, I was excited and looked forward to meeting my dad, who I would later call Papa, and began daydreaming about the wonderful time I would have when I met my dad. I remember overhearing the mention of C.A. in a number of grown-up conversations that I was not a part of but could not recall any of their substance. At the time I had no reason to be curious at the name C.A.

***

Baffoa Lodge sits on top of Jubilee Hill, right behind Jubilee School, a government primary school in Cape Coast. The drive up the winding road to the top of the hill was dramatic but my first impression of entering Baffoa Lodge was that it was a rich man's palatial estate. At the time there were very few homes in the area so it sat alone surrounded by beautiful gardens both in the large front compound and all around the building. I was awestruck by the mountaintop majestic house. Although our home in Suame was lovely and comfortable, this was different. *Whoever lives here must be very rich*, I thought.

We entered the main entrance through this huge alcove that led straight into a magnificent living room beautifully decorated with a grand piano to one side. A large corridor circled the living room with the back side of the corridor facing the Atlantic Ocean. Surrounding the living room were bedrooms, playrooms, and other anterooms.

A grand staircase led to the second floor with another living room above the one below. I found out later that Papa's bedroom and that of his wife, his Mrs., were on the second floor, in addition to other rooms for his children by the Mrs. I would in the course of my stay in Cape Coast get the chance to properly explore the house and to learn more about the people who were part of my dad's life in this place.

There was a third floor to the house with a large outdoor space for parties and my dad's study lined with books on shelves from top to bottom. Everywhere I looked my breath caught in my throat as I took in the panoramic view of Cape Coast, the other hilltops in the city, and the sparkling blue-green Atlantic Ocean below. There was an outside building next to the house where the household help, the gardener, and the driver stayed with their families in their apartments with their own separate kitchen and bath facilities.

***

When my Kumasi entourage arrived, Papa was seated outside on the main balcony facing the main entrance to the house so, of course, he had seen us arrive. He did not get up to meet us. We went upstairs to see him seated in his lounge cane chair on the balcony reading his book. He stood up to shake our hands as was customary.

I muttered a quiet "Good afternoon, Papa," not knowing what else to say.

He shook my hands gently and with a slight smile on his face said, "Seguah, *akwaaba*" (*akwaaba* meaning you are welcome in Akan), then turned to shake Maa's hands. Naana Efua Seguah was my name given at birth, Efua being the name for a girl born on Friday and Seguah was my father's grandmother's name. At home everyone called me Naana, whereas to start school you invariably get an English name and thus I used Emelia at school. Papa addressing me by Seguah felt different, though I loved my name. I had no overwhelming feeling of excitement or joy. It was more a sense of awe as to who he was and why he lived in such a huge house. What was the story behind it? Why had I never met or heard of him before?

I didn't know anything about my father and only learned about him in small bits and pieces. Remember, children in those days did not ask too many questions. You were informed what you needed to know, and from there you moved on.

Papa was pleasant and warm, not effusive. A young girl came and offered us the traditional welcome water, as was customary to offer to anybody who came to visit. We sipped the water as tradition requires. Subsequently, with the traditional Akan welcome custom, Papa followed with the traditional Akan greeting, "You are very welcome. *Akwaaba*. We know and yet we have to ask. What brings you here this afternoon?"

Maa responded, "We bring no bad tidings or evil spirits from Kumasi. We rather bring you warm greetings from the entire family."

She paused for a moment as I listened intently, shifting my eyes from Maa to Papa as they each spoke.

"Emelia has been admitted to Wesley Girls High School," my mother continued, then told him all the preparations she had made to get all my prospectus together. "School is opening today, and we've traveled from Kumasi to the Cape Coast. I'm bringing your daughter to meet you before starting school. I look forward to your oversight of her and her academics while she is close by."

She inquired if it was alright for me to come over to Baffoa Lodge during school short breaks.

"Of course," Papa said.

They talked a while about our travel from Kumasi. He inquired about the health of my brothers, my grandma, and the rest of the family in Kumasi.

"You must study and work hard at school," he added, turning to me.

"*Yoo, Papa, maatse,*" I responded. It means literally, "Okay

Papa, I have heard and understand." I thought perhaps that doing well in school might get me the opportunity to come and stay at this beautiful mansion. I was suddenly longing for an opportunity to see more of this incredibly huge home.

I sat quietly throughout their conversation and said very little, although my mind was preoccupied and fascinated by the house with questions running through my head—how many people live here, and who may they be? Why is the house so quiet with few people visible since we came in? Suame is never quiet. Apart from my dad inquiring directly from me how I was doing, there was not much said between us. I told him I was well with a broad smile on my face, looking expectantly at him as if he was to provide me with something I didn't know I didn't have. There was nothing. He seemed pleasant, and I marveled at the resemblance of my brothers to him. They all looked very much like him. He must have been exactly like them at the age they were now.

How was it possible that I had a father but never heard anything about him till now? That thought kept running through my mind, but children are not supposed to ask such questions so I kept quiet and listened to them chatting until it was time to go. We said our goodbyes, and my dad encouraged me to study hard at school. I already knew that and was determined to do so before I stepped into Baffoa Lodge. His encouragement was added to the stream of the others I had heard from my loved ones and family back in Kumasi.

On my way to school Maa told me more about my father. She informed me that he was a very important person. He was the Vice-Chancellor of the University of Cape Coast, the first one appointed to start this new government sponsored University to join the other two national universities in the country. She was excited about the possibility of me spending more time with him and getting to know him since I was now so close, and she encouraged me to visit the house whenever we had an exeat to go out from the school on Saturday afternoons after all our housework was done and inspections completed.

The excitement was now building—a new school and now I had a dad close by I could spend time with. During our visit my dad informed us that one of my stepsisters, Adelaide, also attended Wesley Girls; she was just a year ahead of me. That was wonderful news. My mind overflowed with information. A new school, a father, and now my own sister. What other pieces of information were out there about my family that I needed to know? How come everything was just coming up now? I was sure I would be able to get the details later. I would ask my mom when the time was right.

Sometimes in life you wonder after events have passed and you reflect and wonder whether there was a right or wrong way of doing things. When you don't have the information to make a judgment one way or the other, you end up going with the flow, learning as you go along, and as you are exposed to different situations that then shed light on past events. I didn't ask my mother much. There was nothing to ask. All I knew was that I had finally met my dad who was a prominent member of society. I was now close to where he was and would have many opportunities to spend time with him. Although I had no need for additional provisions or clothes or money since Maa had ensured I had everything I needed, I knew and looked forward to spending time together with him just like I did with Maa and her side of the family in Kumasi. I hoped it would be another loving and caring environment to grow up in. I was now beyond excited.

CHAPTER 7

If there was a period that tremendously shaped my life both as a student and as an individual person, it was my seven years at Wesley Girls High School. Founded in 1856, Wesley Girls is one of the oldest girls' secondary schools in Ghana and recognized for its excellence in teaching and learning, student support and encouragement, and steeped in the Methodist traditions. It was the number one institution to aim for as a Methodist, and for any girl seeking to excel and pursue further education. That aspiration for young girls in Ghana continues until today.

Emelia at her class reunion of Wesley Girls High School, standing in front of the school statue, "Brainy Beauty," representing an epitome of womanhood.

Wesley Girls High School, home to 600 students, was a dreamland. The taxi we took from Baffoa Lodge arrived at the school gate late in the afternoon. The driver slowly made that right turn onto the long hilly driveway toward the compound. We could see the sports field on the left with well cut grass and patches of brown dirt along the edges. My heart was pumping with excitement, looking to and fro as we passed some homes on both sides of the road before arriving at the main parking lot bustling with students and faculty members waiting to meet and greet the arriving students. The Headmistress, Ms. Clarice Garnett, and the Assistant Headmistress,

Ms. Barbara Bowman, as well as a number of the other adults were at the main parking lot in front of the school compound between the school offices and the Assembly Hall. Many other students had also arrived, and the area was bustling with parents offloading their children and saying their goodbyes. Older students checked student lists and assisted new students in getting to their assigned dormitories and answered their many questions.

There were seven student dormitories. The four older dormitories—Bellamy, Ellis, Waldron, and Wrigley—along with a number of junior classrooms flanked the side of the main gardens and walkway that led directly to the school chapel at its end. I would learn that the long and attractive walkway was affectionately called "*Atra*" —the Fanti name for walkway—by the students. The centrally located chapel with its tall steeple was the main building you saw when entering the school property. The three newer dormitories—Ward Brew, Compton, and Abban—were situated further beyond and behind the chapel. I was assigned to Waldron House.

Senior students assigned to each dormitory led me and other new students into our dormitory, which slept twenty-five students on the top floor of Waldron. Students in Forms 1 to 3 were always assigned to the bigger dorms. Students in Forms 4 and 5 moved to a smaller dormitory with a maximum of six students. In the Form 6 there would only be two students per room.

Those of us who arrived late were met with the warm welcome of other new students who had already settled in, emptied their trunks, and neatly made their beds under the supervision of the seniors. We sat quietly, taking in our new environment and slowly picking up courage to chat with the ones closest to us in hushed tones, not knowing what to do. Before long we would get to know each other very well, grow and learn together, and develop strong friendships that would last a lifetime.

At Wesley Girls and other secondary schools, students would complete Forms 1 to 5 and then sat for the Cambridge General Certificate of Education (GCE) Examination Ordinary Level (O Level). Depending on how well you did at the O-Level, you could then continue to the two-year Lower and Upper Form 6 after which you took the GCE Advanced Level examinations to enter the

University.

Wesley Girls was established in 1836 as a primary school for twenty-five girls by Mrs. Harriet Wrigley, the wife of a British Methodist clergy. According to the history, Wrigley's aim was to give the girls basic training in housekeeping and catechism. The subjects taught at the time included writing, reading, sewing, and religious education. Classes were held at the Manse in the Standfast Hall near the Victoria Park in Cape Coast.

However, Mrs. Wrigley fell ill and died five months after her arrival to the Gold Coast, hence the school was dysfunctional until 1837 when another headmistress, Mrs. Elizabeth Waldron, arrived from the United Kingdom. Waldron steered the affairs of the school for forty-three years, and it morphed into the Wesleyan Girls' School and Training Home. Other headmistresses, teachers, and students followed, making the school one of the most prominent, successful and highly ranked all-girls secondary schools in Ghana and beyond.

Emelia at Wesley Girls School Reunion, standing on "Atra"

My Form 1 class was divided into three separate classes (Junior, Middle, and Senior) based on age with about thirty students each per class. Those of us who were the youngest had just turned twelve and were in the Junior class. The two other classes had older students, becoming secondary school students at thirteen to fourteen years old. Through a thorough orientation in the dormitory by the House Prefect, House Mistress, and subsequent school assemblies, we all began to get a better understanding of the organization and functioning of the school. I had been in boarding schools from a very young age so I was pretty adept in the basic self-sufficiency needed to settle in quickly. Wesley Girls, though, was different in a lot of ways.

Even though I was now older, this was a much bigger institution and was the first school I attended where most of the teachers were white—*Abrofo*, we would call them. Three quarters of the teachers were non-Ghanaian, mostly British, though there were a few from Canada and the United States as well as from Sri Lanka and Southern Rhodesia, currently Zimbabwe.

Each class was assigned a Faculty Leader, and each dormitory had a faculty House Mistress. The house mistress for my house, Waldron, was Ms. Barbara Jennings, who we nicknamed "Sabuu" for her super strict demeanor and unflinching demand for strict obedience of all school rules. She would not tolerate any talking, or even whispering, after the lights out bell went off. We were expected to immediately close our eyes and sleep, which was pretty much impossible for most of us young ones eager to chat and giggle till the seniors went to bed later. The housemistress's key role was to ensure the dormitories were clean and orderly at all times and that there was no loitering and noise after "lights out." Any student found breaking rules was punished with extra gardening work around the dormitory or was made to stand outside at "*Atra*" in the middle of the night and be feasted upon by mosquitoes.

If there was one key lesson we took from Wesley Girls, it was the all-around expectation from faculty and staff that each student was special and each student was expected to excel in both academics and sports. In academics, they knew individual skills varied so there were systems in place to provide the necessary extra tutoring and extra support to any student who needed the help.

Secondary schools bring students together from all walks of life and differing economic and social classes. The level of exposure and academics varied between schools in the cities and those in the rural communities. Whereas some of us had been using microscopes in our biology classes in *Mmofraturo*, for example, there were students who were seeing one for the first time. The goal academically was to ensure that each student attained their maximum potential regardless of where they came from. There was genuine interest in each individual's growth and progress throughout their academic tenure at the school. There was encouragement, support, and praise when you made the necessary effort. You were reprimanded when you didn't achieve the potential the teachers saw in you, and they would do whatever was needed for each and every one of us in spite of our childhood mischief and naughtiness.

We had teachers from all over the world. In reality, the majority of the teachers were from the United Kingdom and North America. There was Ms. Moss, our mathematics teacher, Ms. Brinkworth, for French, Miss Jennings for biology, and a number of others from the United Kingdom. Ms. Gall, an elderly British woman, also played the piano for morning worship, and we would change the words of the songs sometimes just to irritate her. There was Mrs. Wickrema, our geography teacher from Sri Lanka who also taught us to play tennis; Ms. Datta from India who taught history; and Mrs. Lindsay from Southern Rhodesia, now Zimbabwe, who also taught geography and was married to a Ghanaian. We were always in awe of the saris worn by Ms. Datta and Mrs. Wickrema, as well as their graceful manners. We had a couple of other teachers from Canada, Mr. and Mrs. Spedding taught chemistry and literature, respectively, and Mr. Jack Arn taught economics. We also had a few Ghanaian staff members including Ms. Wood for commerce, Mrs. Acquaye-Badoo for art, Ms. Koramoa, our school nurse, and Ms. Hughes for physical education,

Ms. Tewiah was an English teacher for some classes, and for me she taught my local language, Fanti, as well. She was nicknamed *Kaansa*, meaning "even if or though" in Fanti. Reportedly, many years before I was at the school, she had punished some students who completely ignored her by turning their back to her. She turned around and in her classic Fanti said "*kaansa meye onyimpa mpo a,*" meaning even though I am a person talking to you, you ignored me. She gained a permanent nickname.

CHAPTER 8

We could be naughty at times in giving all our teachers nicknames, which made them angry, I remember the time in music class when our teacher, Ms. Marilyn Diamond from England, was conducting the music and moving her hands up and down. She wore a rather long black skirt and a lovely white top, which was a bit see-through. With one big move up of her hands, we saw her right breast falling out below her bra. That was the end of the lesson. The entire class burst into laughter, and no matter how much she screamed at us we could not stop laughing. Needless to say, we found ourselves at the end of the school day spaced out on "*Atra*" for over two hours as punishment. We still laugh about this each time we meet when someone remembers and brings it up. It did not deter Ms. Diamond from still enfolding us with her warmth and love in the days and years after.

We would often gang up in delaying handing in our geography homework, and Mrs. Lindsay would be so mad at us. She often told us she wondered how we would manage as adults. She felt we were so lazy; all we wanted was to press some light switch for all our needs to be met. We used to laugh so much when she said things like that, and now we are literally touching switches to do a lot for us. Who would have thought that was possible?

***

Time goes by quickly when you are having fun. The secondary school years went by quickly. On top of our academic work, we practiced sports, volunteered with a Workcamp group, assisted the Red Cross when it visited Kakumdo, the village next to our school to nurse wounds and feed the children, and joined the Girl Scouts. With these and other extracurricular activities, we were busy at school. Midterms and final exam times came by so quickly each term. I was very happy and content at school. I had made a lot of friends in my year group and in my dormitory, spending our free time braiding each other's hair or gossiping about one student or teacher or the other as adolescents do.

I would write letters home to my mom and brothers and also to my dad and would wait anxiously to hear back from them. I do not recall my dad visiting me in school, but he would reply to my letters and ask how I was doing. Once I received a postcard from him with a picture of the Empire State Building. He said he had gone to New York City for a meeting. I was so excited. All my classmates saw and read his message. I felt so very important, knowing New York City was across the Atlantic Ocean and thus very far away.

Letters were always distributed at the beginning of the evening study period so everyone could see who had received mail. We knew all there was to know about each other's families and friends and shared a lot among ourselves. We would read each other's letters and tease those who appeared not to be getting any letters. Our class had a lot of mischievous girls, and we cracked jokes among ourselves all the time. We studied hard, too, helped each other with assignments, and studied together often, ensuring that we were all doing well. This camaraderie extended beyond school. On holidays, those in any one city, village, or town would socialize during the break and spend a lot of time together at home as well. We therefore grew up to become a strong network of very good supportive friends spread all over the world.

I would occasionally spend time with my cousin Minnette in her Bellamy House with her friends who would all pamper me and encourage me to continue to study hard. They had heard and seen that I was doing well in school since I would get a few prizes during the annual speech and prize giving days. I seldom saw my half-sister, Adelaide. Even when I went to her dormitory to see one of my classmates and I saw her, we acted like we lived on different planets and barely spoke to each other.

I enjoyed studying, doing well, and getting good grades. I worked as hard as I could in all my classes. I sought help from my teachers, when needed, and studied with my friends and classmates in my dormitory. Takyiwaa Manuh, Mercy Acquaah, and others including Adowaba Korsah who was in a different dormitory were my study mates. I spent a lot of free time with my other close friend Vicky Wireko in Abban house. Vicky and I were in Form 4 when we were able to go out for exeat on Saturday afternoons after homework and dormitory inspections were done; we would go to Cape Coast together to the Kotokoraba market to buy provisions and just hang out in town for a while. Her dad had a friend who owned a provisions shop so we would go to see him and he would send us back to school with bottles of Fanta and Coca Cola and biscuits. Those were special Saturdays.

One of those Saturdays when we were let out early, I decided I would go home to see Papa and spend the afternoon with his family instead of the market with Vicky. I was so sure I would bring a lot of provisions back to school from my dad's house. I took the local *"trotro"* transport from the school gate, which dropped me off at the main lorry station at Kotokoraba market. I took another *"trotro"* and was dropped off at Jubilee school and climbed the hill happily to Baffoa Lodge.

As always Papa was sitting on his balcony on the second floor reading the newspaper. I did not see anyone on the ground floor that day so I climbed up the stairs and went straight to Papa. He welcomed me, and I sat with him for almost an hour. He quizzed me about how I was doing in school, the teachers, and the food. He informed me he had been receiving my school reports at the end of each term and I was doing very well. I needed to keep my head down and keep working hard. He was sure I would be able to enter the University when I completed the Form 6 examinations. He encouraged me to listen to the teachers and ensure my homework was always done on time. It seemed like we chatted forever. That was the first time the two of us sat alone and chatted with no one else around. I had already been at Wesley Girls for over three years, only seeing him briefly whenever I went over to the house before school reopened and to say goodbye at the end of the school year as I left for holidays in Kumasi.

That day, after we had chatted for a while he told me my older stepsister, Nancy Ackah, was home on a break from her secondary boarding school in Mampong, near Kumasi, and she would make sure I had some food to eat before going back to school. Another sister? How many of them were there? He called Nancy and asked her to take me to greet her mother who was busy cooking in the kitchen. I literally jumped and almost fell down when I saw Nancy. I looked exactly like her except that she was taller and, of course, much older. The resemblance was stunning even in my young eyes. At home she was called Maame Aba, the name for a girl born on Tuesday. She took me toward the kitchen at the back of the house. As we made the bend, I could already smell the aroma of the food, reminding me of Maa's kitchen and the warmth that always exuded from there. We entered and saw the woman of the house seated on her big stool busy stirring the stew in the large cast iron pot on the coal pot in the kitchen. There was a smiling young girl helping her. I smiled back at the young sweet girl. My excitement started to boil. I happily greeted her, ensuring I ended with an emphatic "Maa." The woman on the stool barely lifted her head to look at me or to acknowledge my presence.

I greeted her again, much louder, in case she had not heard. There was absolutely no response. At that point Maame Aba beckoned me to come along, and I followed her numbly with my head down. I instinctively felt that this woman disliked me, maybe was even disgusted by me. It struck me then that this must be the first time I had met someone who absolutely did not appear interested in me. Did I do something wrong? I had said nothing except share a proper greeting and curtsy like I had always done for other grown-ups. Was there something else I was supposed to say? I was used to all the grown-ups, even strangers, in Suame, in all my schools and in the market with Maame Yaa,

Emelia at entrance to Wesley Girls School

who were always happy to see me. This woman was different. I made a mental note of her.

I followed Maame Aba everywhere she went. When we were

finally settled and seated in her bedroom, I had to ask. I was overcome with worry and anxiety.

"Who was that woman in the kitchen?" I said hesitantly. "Did I do something wrong?"

Maame Aba heaved a huge sigh and sat still for a minute.

"That is my mom," she said. "Do you see my sister Adelaide at school?"

"No," I told her Adelaide doesn't talk to me or respond to me when I go to see my classmates in her dormitory.

Maame Aba told me that she had other brothers who I would meet perhaps the next time I came to visit. I did not stay for long that day. Maame Aba got some lunch for me, which we ate quietly together, and after I said goodbye to Papa on the balcony, I went back down the hill and up the road. I decided to clear my head by walking to Kotokoraba to take the *trotro* back to school instead of taking the second *trotro*.

This started my periodic visits to Baffoa Lodge. During my next visit, I followed the same routine. This time, however, I entered Baffoa Lodge and walked the short corridor to the winding stairs. At the very top of these long stairs sat a huge black cat staring directly at me. I shuddered with fear. I put an additional bounce in my step and hurriedly walked past the cat to the veranda. The cat did not budge an inch. I sat with Papa for a while as usual until, out of nowhere, Adelaide appeared to put cushions on some of the chairs. She said something to Papa that I did not quite hear and barely noticed my presence. Papa asked if I played with Adelaide at school sometimes. I remember looking at him as if to say is that a real question? I slowly shared with Papa the fact that Adelaide and I did not spend any time together in school. I seldom saw her. I thought to myself how nice it would be to have a sister so that we could have come home together and have a lot of fun. That was never to be.

Maame Aba was not home but the young helper in the house came to call me to eat before going back to school. I sat with her in the corridor. We talked in low tones to each other as if we were scared of being overhead by anyone. This sweet young girl of about eleven years was called Seguah.

"Seguah is my name, too," I said.

We had both been named after my great grandmother,

Maame Baffoa's mother. She was not a house girl, but Papa's daughter from another woman. Her mom lived not far from Baffoa Lodge but she seldom got to see her. She would be thoroughly beaten if she were to go there.

I finished eating and was ready to head back to school. I said goodbye to Papa and went on my way. As if I had not seen enough for the day, I lingered a while in the Kotokoraba market. Just about the time I got off my *trotro* at the school gate to walk up the road to my campus, I saw Papa's longtime driver, Smiler, driving Adelaide back to school in Papa's Mercedes-Benz. Smiler waved and drove on. Adelaide sat in the back seat motionless.

It was as if a padding had been removed from my eyes. I was distraught. I sat at the edge of the school sports field at the school entrance and cried my heart out. I finally got some energy to get up and walk slowly back to my dorm with my head down. To have been in the house at the same time and for Papa to have just left me to walk and take the *trotro* back to school when he knew the driver would take Adelaide to the same school. Even in my little girl's mind something was wrong.

It finally hit me. I was not considered their equal. If that's how Papa was going to treat me, I decided I would no longer go to Baffoa Lodge. What was the point of going only to be there and be humiliated? I was a complete unwelcome stranger in that house. I never felt any real joy. I was longing to develop the deep and strong relationship with Papa as I had with Maa. But now I also realized that he did not care a hoot about me or was unable to care about me. Either way I didn't need to spend my energy looking up to him. What kind of father would have two children in the same school and send his driver to pick one up to bring home and allow the other to take a *trotro* to come to the same house? Even if he didn't know I was coming to the house, he could have had me return in the car with his favorite daughter. To date, I cannot understand why Papa behaved the way he did.

I will not hazard a guess, but I believe that there was nothing he could not have done if he himself sincerely wanted to treat me like a real daughter. It cannot solely be attributed to a fear of his wife.

Suddenly, all the pieces came together. Why was the black cat following me all around Baffoa Lodge from the time I came in till I left each and every single time? I remembered childhood stories from Elmina about witches parading as black cats. Why was the woman in the house so unwelcoming to me? I had had enough of Baffoa Lodge. To me it was never home and never felt like one.

Over time, and with me asking questions wherever I could, I began to piece a few things together. It would be years before I could get the entire package of the family history. But for now, I knew Papa had children with a lot of other women. The woman in Baffoa Lodge had eight children, six boys and the two girls. Over the period I was at Wesley Girls, I met all of them except the eldest son who was in England studying medicine. My mom had the four of us, three boys and me. I met my younger stepsister Seguah. I had an older step-sister, Mrs. Agnes Dzidzienyo, from another woman who was a midwife and lived in Accra with her husband, Edwin. When Papa's Mrs. died, he remarried, and there were three more siblings with her. I suspected there were other children out there, yet to be discovered.

Emelia in Suame

It was much later when I learned that prominent men, in fact, a lot of men, had many women with whom they had children and maintained their households. I also learned that some men would bring all the children together and take care of all of them. For individuals married under the Ghana Marriage Act like Papa, polygamy was not an allowed practice in law but it was very common. Papa was not one of those to provide reasonably for all his children even though he had the means to do so. I recalled an experience of my younger brother, Nana Apreh. He was then at Mfantsipim School, a boys' secondary school also in Cape Coast. His school sandals broke, and he urgently needed a replacement. He went to Baffoa Lodge to ask Papa for money to buy a new pair at the Bata shop in town. Instead of giving him the five pounds (equivalent to ten dollars at the time), Papa went into his bedroom and brought a pair of his own old shoes for Nana. Nana took the shoes and threw them away on his way back to school. He borrowed from other students until my mom bought new ones from Kumasi for him. Needless to say, Nana never set foot at Baffoa Lodge again.

***

That summer when I went back home to Suame, I knew who exactly to talk to about the events in Cape Coast. I talked to Maa, to Maame Yaa, and lastly to my grandma Maame Ama Atta. They all acknowledged my pain and told me not to worry about it. They reassured me of their love and the importance of knowing that I would never be in want so long as they were alive. What stayed with me was what my grandmother did a couple of days later. She called me to come sit with her and play the game *Oware*. We played for a while and then she stopped to chat.

"I have heard about what happened at Baffoa Lodge," she said. "You are still a child with many years ahead of you. What happened at your father's house, take as a life lesson. Not everyone you meet will like you or, in fact, adore you as your family and close friends do. That is life. You cannot spend your life worrying about other people's reactions. What is important is for you to learn to be good to all the people you meet and do not let them bring you down."

As we finished the game, she told me *"Se obi se wu a, nya nkwa kyere no,"* which is an Akan proverb meaning "If someone wants you to die you need to live beyond their expectations for them to see." That proverb has never been far from my thoughts, and I have remembered and tried to live by it throughout my life.

***

No one told me not to go back to Baffoa Lodge but in my own heart I did not see the value of going through all the hassle to go there from school when I would rather happily be hanging out with my friends in the market at Kotokoraba or we could spend the time lazily walking on the Kakumdo road all the way to the next village, Abura, to buy coconuts and roasted plantains and peanuts. I was truly content doing that. I was well fed at school. When needed, I had all the provisions I needed in my chop box. I internalized within me that I would not miss the time spent with Papa on his balcony talking about school and the importance of education. I never went back to Baffoa Lodge again for years.

CHAPTER 9

Wesley girls turned out to be much more exciting and enriching than I ever envisaged. In addition to academics, I was introduced to a broad range of extracurricular activities. I learned to play tennis well, and Mrs. Wickrema, who was both our geography teacher and our tennis coach, was extremely supportive. The

Emelia with her year-group at their
fiftieth reunion at Wesley Girls in 2020

importance of community service was ingrained in us. I joined the Voluntary Workcamps group, the Red Cross, and the Girl Scouts.

All these activities broadened my horizon about the world around me and exposed me to the level of poverty in the villages right around our school including Abura and Kakumdo. I could tangibly see the appreciation of the small efforts we were making to support these villages.

The young children would surround us and seek to be the first ones we attended to when we went with the Red Cross on health days. We cleaned and bandaged their wounds, and they would sit attentively and listen to us when we taught them about the importance of cleanliness, washing hands, sweeping their compounds, and brushing their teeth.

These activities also provided an opportunity for me to develop lifelong relationships with my school friends, classmates, and those from other classes who were part of my teams. This has continued to be a sisterhood I can count on at any time. As much as we bonded on many fronts, there were other times when I would feel detached and preferred to stay on my own to watch what was going on around me. Although I was sociable and enjoyed the company of my friends, I also learned to find solace in being alone. At home in Suame there were many times I felt alone in spite of the bustling activities in our house. I enjoyed the solitude as it gave me an opportunity to observe people and discern some of the complexities of the relationships around me.

One of the areas that was of keen interest but I was not able to pursue was the study of piano. You needed to have a piano at home to be able to have piano lessons. Although Papa had two pianos in Baffoa Lodge, that was not my home; he never offered piano lessons, although I often heard Adelaide practicing. Again, the differentiation stared me in the face. It truly hurt, but it was beyond my control so I tried to push the thought aside whenever it came to mind.

In addition to activities at Wesley Girls, there were numerous opportunities to interact with students from other secondary schools in Cape Coast, which was a center of education. There were many secondary schools including Mfantsipim School, Adisadel, and St. Augustine's, which were all-boys schools, Holy Child School, an all-girls school, and Aggrey Memorial, which was co-educational, and others. There were always intercollegiate athletics and debating societies. Students from different schools would join to work together on other voluntary projects. We developed friendships across schools with the highlights occurring when any girl received a letter from a boy during study time.

We would all wait to hear the contents of each person's letter. I remember the evenings when literally the entire class anxiously waited for someone to receive a letter from a new boyfriend in Mfantsipim or any of the other schools. When a letter arrived, we would all make noise and insist she read it aloud. Some of the commotion and noise around this sometimes led to *Atra* punishment from Ms. Jennings but we could not resist. It was a lot of fun.

At times the girls' gossip was wild. Once word got around that some Wesley Girls students had been seen with some boys making out behind some rock mound after our intercollegiate sports. We were all wild and fascinated, trying to figure out who these girls and boys were. This gossip and mystery would last for semesters.

The expectation from all the teachers, staff, and school seniors for the juniors was that we would excel in whatever areas we needed. I worked very hard on my studies to ensure I did well in the exams especially for the General Certificate Examinations (GCE) Ordinary Level. This examination was organized by the University of Cambridge and a good grade ensured access to the two-year Advanced Level program. Just as for the screening examinations at *Mmofraturo* into secondary school, a failure in this examination meant you could not attend a tertiary institution. The options then were to attend a teacher training institution or any of the technical polytechnics in the country. For some reason, I had put in my mind that I would work hard and become a doctor. To do this, I did need to go to medical school. There was no question; I had to do well to get into the A-Level program.

Luckily, in July 1969 I received the notification of my passing all the nine subjects offered for the GCE O-Level exam. I did very well on both the science and the arts subjects but my mind was already made up to pursue science on my way to the medical career I had been dreaming of. Hooray, I was on my way to my lifelong dream. My Form 6 courses would include biology, chemistry, and physics as well as the general studies course mandatory for all Form

6 students.

My excitement and joy were tempered a bit, though. I was not going to be able to share my exuberance with my favorite grandmother who had always propped me up and comforted me through my sorrows and pains. The year before, I was suddenly called to the office of Ms. Garnett. A call to the office of the headmistress is never welcome. It had to be important. I did not recall any recent naughtiness in the past, bad enough for Ms. Jennings to report me to the Headmistress. What could the call be about?

I went down to the office with a lot of apprehension, and I saw Minnette had also been called to the office. *It must be something from home*, I thought, getting more nervous. Ms. Garnett, however, was very friendly and in her usual motherly mood that day. She sat us down and after a few pleasantries informed us of the telephone call she had received about the sudden passing of our grandmother, Maame Amma Atta. We both burst into tears and were inconsolable.

She let our tears subside before informing us of the plans that had been made for us to go back to Kumasi for the funeral. We would leave school a few days before the official end of the term. Until then Minnette and I would get together from time to time and reminisce about Maame. We would recall some of her favorite sayings and proverbs and cry more each time. One of my favorites that Minnette did not like was *"Minnette mbu dweetee* ("Minnette has no respect for money") as she spends the money recklessly when she goes to the market.

Maame Ama Atta was a true anchor in my life and upbringing. She was a gentle, loving, and warm soul, steeped in the spirit of Methodism. Maame was an elder in the Kumasi Central Methodist Church, a lifelong leader of one of the small groups in the church supporting others in their faith and discipleship journeys. She was a cherished member of her church community. She never went to school but in all aspects she was more educated than those who had been. She was a trader in the Kumasi Kejetia market. Her market stall was filled with the barrels of smoked tobacco she sold, and you would often see her with a lump of it in her cheek during the day. She knew and cared for her customers who came from all over the Ashanti and Brong Ahafo regions to purchase in bulk from her to sell in their small shops in the villages. She knew I loved *"apiti,"* which was a snack made from pounded ripe plantain, seasoned with pepper, ginger, salt, and baked in plantain leaves. It was delicious. She would make sure she had some waiting for me whenever I visited her in the market during my school holiday breaks.

Sundays would see her in the main Kumasi Methodist Church as a staunch member of the Singing Band, which was then mostly composed of choristers who were unable to read. Her solos were heard during the three-hour Sunday services. As a lay leader whose house was a short walk to the Church, she participated in many service programs, including providing needed support to young ministers who were transferred to our Kumasi Circuit. It was in this regard that she and the Rev. and Mrs. Joseph DeGraft-Johnson met and became lifelong family friends. In fact, it was Rev. DeGraft-Johnson who went with Maa and me to Elmina to start my boarding school experience.

Maame cheered me on through each and every achievement and reminded me numerous times of the importance of hard work, knowing that our Good Lord was always with me. I believed her and trusted her every word.

She apparently had fallen in the bathroom and hit her head on the floor. After being rushed to the Okomfo Anokye Hospital, the main hospital in Kumasi, unconscious, she remained in a coma for three days before passing away. Her funeral was the first of a family member that I saw, and I was awed both at the mournful nature of loss and also by the immense celebrations around death to send off loved ones with pomp and ceremony. For weeks before the funeral, the house at Kejetia was filled with family and friends from around the country, dressed in the traditional black cloth, sitting for hours on end with the family. The family organized the customary overnight wake-keeping in the house the day before the funeral. The whole neighborhood was full of well-wishers who had come to bid her farewell. There was no room both inside and outside the house. On the day of the funeral, an emotional service was held for her at the Methodist Church followed with the burial at the Tafo cemetery. The customary after-burial durbar was held on the large field in front of her house with well-wishers entertained with cultural drumming and dancing to celebrate her life with refreshments served throughout the rest of the day. Funerals in Ghana, I learnt, were major events in the Ghanaian community.

***

The two years in Form 6 went by like a breeze. We had more liberties. I shared a room with my good friends Takyiwaa Manuh and Eva Lokko. We had the option to go to town every Saturday if we wanted and, of course, lights off was closer to 10 p.m. One assumed that with three main subjects of study as opposed to the nine for O-Level, the burden would be lighter. It was not. Our teachers—Mr. Spedding for chemistry, Ms. Jennings for biology, and Mr. Griffiths for physics—ensured we had our plates full with practicals, independent and team assignments, quizzes, and reading. We still made time to attend school dances when the boys came from other secondary schools. On Saturdays we would walk to Abura to buy coconuts or idle in the dorm braiding our hair in the exotic styles only allowed for Form 6 students.

Before long we were done with exams and eagerly awaiting the results. To top it off, those of us who lived in Kumasi did not take the usual buses home. Instead, we went to the harbor town of Takoradi and spent the day gallivanting with our friends from the Sekondi-Takoradi area, sightseeing and having a good time. In the evening we took the sleeper train from Takoradi to Kumasi. We thoroughly enjoyed the well-appointed sleeper train with meals. We sang and danced till we could barely stand. We woke up the next morning at the Kumasi train station.

I had entered Wesley Girls seven years earlier with a lot of energy and excitement, and I was leaving fulfilled in ways I could never have dreamt of. I had been near the top of my class for the entire seven years, been appreciated and encouraged by all around me, and had made a lot of very good friends along the way. I had achieved academically and socially and been empowered to face whatever came ahead with confidence. I could only see a rosy road ahead.

CHAPTER 10

I was back in Suame after all the end-of-school celebrations. I was busy dreaming about finally getting my wish to wear the white laboratory coat that the qualified medical students wore, with Dr. Ackah neatly embossed on the pocket. Oh, what a day that would be! My entire family and my teachers had cheered me on, and there was no doubt in anyone's mind that I would do well and move on from Wesley Girls to the University of Ghana Medical School, the country's foremost University at Legon in Accra. My excitement and anxiety overflowed as the July results date drew near.

When it finally arrived, it did not turn out as I had planned. I received a grade of C in the Physics A-Level examination and was therefore not going to be admitted to the Medical School. My whole world shattered. I sat on a small stool next to the small television at the corner of our living room in Suame, the curtain next to me pulled to cover my face as I cried uncontrollably for hours. I cried till I could cry no more. I was filled with utter shame for disappointing all the people who had trusted me to do well. I was completely lost. What would become of me? Perhaps I had not studied enough? I should have stayed all the time with the books instead of having fun with my friends. I had ignored opportunities.

But most important, what could I do now? I was a complete failure. I was unable to think or eat or drink. I could only cry.

"Don't worry; there are other things you can do," Maa told me again and again. "I will talk to my friends at the different universities, and we will find other options for you."

I could not hear or feel anything beyond my pain and deep disappointment. Maame should have been here; she would have enfolded me in her love and made everything good.

I spent the next two weeks sobbing between Maa's house and Maame Yaa's house and back again, not knowing what to do with myself. One Thursday afternoon, Yaw Adu-Poku came by the house. Yaw was the son of Mr. and Mrs. Yaw Poku, very good friends of my mom, and he was also my older brother Kodwo's classmate from Achimota Secondary School. Yaw was in his second year at the Ghana Medical School in Accra. Of course, he came to find me still crying and mourning the loss of what could have been. He sat with me for a while and tried to console me but I did not hear anything he said. My mom tried to get me to drink some soup with some warm bread. I barely tasted it.

As Yaw was about to leave, the two of them came and sat with me in my now well-established corner by the television set. Yaw told me about other people he knew in medical school who had not received the best grades for the A-Level the first time around and had been admitted after retaking the A-Level examination and were now doing well. He informed me that the University of Cape Coast, where Papa was the first Vice-Chancellor, had recently started a one-year Preliminary Science program for students who needed to study and retake the A-Level examination. Passing the courses at Cape Coast would enable me to reapply for the medical school the following year.

They both assured me that was a possible option for consideration. My mom said she would reach out to the university and check on the application possibilities since the deadlines were long past. She was hopeful that, with my last name, I could get special consideration if there were still any openings available in the Preliminary Science program. All night long I mulled over the conversation. Could this be a real alternative path for me? What if it did not work out?

My mom jumped into action. By the next day she had contacted the university Registrar through some Order of Odd Fellows Lodge friends and plans were underway for us to visit the University of Cape Coast. There was absolutely no energy or excitement for this trip back to Cape Coast. After an overnight visit and the completion of all the necessary paperwork, we headed back to Kumasi. Within a week, we received the confirmation of my admission to the one-year program. At this point I had no choice and was completely resigned to it. Over the course of the rest of the summer break, I began to actually look forward to it. I had nothing to lose.

The one year spent at the University of Cape Coast turned out to be challenging but very rewarding. I made some very good friends including Veronica Brobbey and Alberta Bodom. I knew what my priority was so I focused on my studies as much as was feasible. Most of the material covered was the same as I had covered in Form

6 so overall it was more of a thorough review than learning from scratch but I took everything in and did very well.

On the social front a lot was brewing. Vero had a boyfriend, Kwaku, who was one of the managers at the Kingsway store in Cape Coast. He would come over on weekends and take us to some of the restaurants in Cape Coast or Elmina, and he would always ensure we had loads of provisions on hand at school.

During the Easter break in 1972, I decided to go to Accra and spend a couple of weeks with my cousin Edith, who worked for the Bank of Ghana. She lived in Kaneshie, one of the Accra suburbs, just a five-minute walk to my friend Vicky Wireko's house. That was a godsend. We spent most of our days together relaxing. In the afternoons we would walk over to the nearby GNTC department store and buy some ice cream and biscuits, then loiter back home savoring each bite. We had a great time together.

Our routine took a different turn one day when I woke up feeling unwell and completely exhausted. I had started complaining of tiredness the day before when we went out to the shop but did not think much of it. Within a day or so I developed a rash all over my body. My cousin suspected it could be chickenpox but could not be sure. The itchy rash was covered with calamine lotion to help ease the pain but still, I could not take it anymore; I was scratching all over. The next morning I woke up early to go to the Korle Bu Teaching Hospital to be examined. As usual the clinic was full of patients, and I had to wait for over two hours before I was even able to get a card made out for me to see the doctor. Yes, the doctor confirmed it was chicken pox and prescribed some calamine lotion and other medications.

By the time I left the hospital I was completely out of it. To get the *trotro* back to Kaneshie I had to walk across the hospital, past the children's hospital and the mortuary, to get to the main road for the *trotro*. I was exhausted and completely drained. I decided to hitchhike to the main road. I did not walk for long, and I saw a small white car approaching. I raised my hand, beckoned in the direction of the main road, and prayed the driver would stop.

He did and asked me where I was going. I requested to be dropped on the main road for the *trotro* to Kaneshie. I am not sure what he saw but he said he would drop me off at home at Kaneshie. He told me I appeared too unwell to walk. I could see a very compassionate look in his eyes. We did not talk much but he asked how I was feeling and how long I had had the rash. Before we could get into any long conversation we were at the house. He dropped me off, wished me well, and said he would check on me another time. I thanked him profusely and headed home to shower and get into bed. I could not go back to school until I was well. Vicky would come by and sit with me each day trying to cheer me up.

In time I started feeling better and was looking forward to Cape Coast again. Two days before I left, we were sitting outside the house on the compound relaxing when someone knocked and came in. No one seemed to know him. It took a bit for me to remember that it was the same gentleman who had given me a ride from the hospital, coming over to check on me as he had promised. How sweet. I introduced him to my cousin and another friend who was visiting with her. He informed us that his name was Albert Timpo. I got up, went to see him off to his car, and told him I was feeling much better and would be going back to school in a couple of days. We spoke outside for a short while, and he suggested we sit at a café across the street from the house, which we did. That turned out to be a two-hour outing.

Scarcely did I guess that was to be a major turning point in my life. After he left I immediately went over to Vicky's house to chitchat about the young Korle Bu doctor who had come back to the house to check on me and had promised to visit when I went back to Cape Coast as well. The evening went on with a lot of excitement.

The year went by quickly for my program at Cape Coast. As the last semester moved along, we heard rumors about the tightening of admission requirements for the Ghana medical school. The University, starting that year, was only to make its student selection from candidates who had successfully received the required grades from the first sitting of the A-Level. Candidates completing the Preliminary program I was enrolled in would no longer be considered unless there were additional vacancies.

I was devastated. How could this be? I had worked so hard, received top grades in all my classes, and was assured I would be able to be admitted to the medical school. Now the rules change meant I had wasted a year when I could have been enrolled somewhere else. All my other colleagues who did not do as well as I did in the Form 6 exam were already at the University of Ghana and the University of Science and Technology in Kumasi, enrolled in other science disciplines such as biochemistry or pharmacy. I could have done that, too. Regret overwhelmed me for a second time in my short life. Was I going to face one setback after another in my life? What was to become of me? Would I end up as a village teacher somewhere? I was completely torn.

Whenever my mom gets herself into action, a new dawn arrives. I was keenly learning from her. She listened carefully to me when I was able to get her on the phone with the news about the admission changes in the medical school. She tried as much as she could to encourage me not to lose hope. Her usual refrain was "When one door closes, the Good Lord opens another one. You only have to pay attention to where you are being directed." She said she would discuss the situation with her Lodge colleagues from different universities and seek their expert guidance.

We followed up with several conversations. By the time I went back home at the end of the academic year I was all set to start a four-year degree program in Agricultural Science at the Kwame Nkrumah University of Science and Technology (KNUST) in Kumasi. I was beginning to accept the fact that life throws you curves when you least expect it so I needed to learn to adapt to move forward. I felt my grandma would also have approved of my thinking had she been around, and that was good enough for me.

I spent a month of the summer break with the national Voluntary Workcamps group traveling to the impoverished northern part of the country, to the small town of Jirapa. The diversion was very welcome. The town council had decided to build a real block building as the new classroom for the local authority school. Until now, the classroom had been located in a thatched shed, which had been built ages ago. That meant that with the arrival of the rainy season each year's classes were suspended and children stayed home, helping parents on farms and deprived from learning.

Young students from other institutions across the country had come to work on this project. We worked hard very early in the morning, starting from dawn to avoid the midday intense one hundred and twenty degrees heat, which made it difficult to do much later in the day. It was a group of about thirty students the month I was there, led and directed by the northern region head of the Voluntary Workcamps program. We considered it fun work, singing as we laid the bricks and put down the mortar or help on the carpentry work, among other things.

We explored the area around us on the weekends, getting on the *trotro* to see the crocodile farm at Paga, a tiny village at the border with Upper Volta, now Burkina Faso, or visiting the market in the region's major town of Lawra on market days when all the farmers from the entire area brought produce to sell.

Market days were festive occasions when relations and friends from neighboring villages would gather to swap gossip, share the information about the latest births, deaths, marriages, and general information on how various farms were thriving or dying. We used our little pocket money to buy raffia baskets and other northern wares to take back home for family and friends. Everyone who could afford one in the region had a bicycle. I could count the total number of cars I saw during the period I was based in Jirapa. Bikes, however, were everywhere. One of the foremen and his friends at the site had bikes so they volunteered to teach some of us how to ride. That was exciting. We would ride through the town late in the evening just before the sun went down and the temperature had cooled from the afternoon heat. It was hilarious, and we were soon to experience one of the memorable occurrences of our stay.

One evening we were riding home when another bike rider came past carrying a huge python wrapped in a basket behind his bike. We all started screaming. The foreman later explained that snakes were a real delicacy in the region so he was sure there was going to be a big family gathering organized in that man's household. We were suddenly glad our stay was almost over.

By the time our group left, the building had progressed to the lintels, then roofing and plastering completed. We had made some good friends and enjoyed the northern hospitality of our hosts who had taught us about their local cultures and foods and ensured we were well taken care of during our entire stay. Most of the staple foods in the northern part of the country were made from millet or sorghum, which grew locally. They would use these grains to make puddings, cakes, and different kinds of soups. I had had enough of the local *"tuo-zafi,"* the local dish made from millet, which was the staple in the region and served with leafy soups, of which the most popular was *"oyoyo,"* made from baobab leaves. A new life awaited me at home, and I was looking forward to it.

Emelia with Vicky and Nora at WGHS.

CHAPTER 11

I was looking forward to going to KNUST, affectionately referred to by all as "Tech." This university was named after Ghana's first president, Dr. Kwame Nkrumah, and a huge sculpture of the president greeted everyone as they entered the main entrance to the elaborate campus. It was the second largest of the three national universities at the time, the other two being the University of Ghana at Legon and the University of Cape Coast.

The major focus of its programs was in the sciences with the exception of a large Art Department offering courses in drawing and sculpture and one program in social science, which had just been initiated. I had been to the campus several times before this time because my youngest brother, Nana Apreh, had attended the University Primary School there, and we had been there to visit family friends over the years. After a year at the University of Cape Coast I enjoyed my classes and living on a university campus. It was not medical school but it was okay, and I was looking forward to new experiences. I was learning to welcome change and its inevitable and unpredictable course. Life's challenges could be overcome, and I was looking forward to experiences that are different from one's initial expectations. It would be well. Little did I know.

The campus was just a thirty-minute drive from home, when there wasn't the usual traffic jam. With traffic around the airport roundabout and Zongo Junction, it could be hours. The first couple of weeks passed as a breeze with me reconnecting with old friends. A few of my Wesley Girls classmates who had started the university directly from Form 6 were there, including Irene Osam-Tewiah. There were other Wesley Girls seniors I knew very well also at Tech taking courses in pharmacy, biochemistry, and architecture among others. Having grown up in Kumasi it was also great to meet other family friends who had been admitted to different programs at Tech including Felicity Adu-Acheampong and Regina Ohene-Darko. Felicity's mom was also a midwife in Kumasi so we had known each other from our time together at *Mmofraturo,* and now we were both enrolled at the same university. Felicity had attended the Holy Child Secondary School also in Cape Coast, and Regina was at Aburi

Secondary School in the Eastern Region. Felicity and I became roommates for our first year. I was not a stranger at Tech.

Everyone on campus marveled at my agriculture cohort. A program that generally had one, or at most two women each year, suddenly had ten of us in the cohort of thirty-five first-year students. Apart from Regina, I knew no one else. It was a collection of students who had come from a broad spectrum of secondary schools, from all walks of life, and from across all regions of the country— each with his or her own life story to share. As we settled in for this four-year program, we were all unsure how this new crop of ladies in the agriculture program would manage. With accomplished lecturers including Drs. Baafour-Senkyire, Osafo, Kankam, and Anim-Yeboah among others, they made it clear to us at the outset that nothing but excellence was expected of us. We soon realized they meant every word. Expectations were very high but all of them were readily accessible for us to go back and meet them for further studies and tutorials. When lectures got very difficult for most students, they would organize additional sessions for review and further discussions.

In a very short time, we bonded and became a cohesive group. I studied with Regina, Janet Aikins, Ohenese Sakyi, and George Koranteng. All the ladies were housed together at the Africa Hall residence, the tall eight-story building near the University shopping center and the Building and Roads Department, with ready access to the village of Ayigya for transport home or to town whenever needed. It was, however, a thirty-minute fast walk to the Agriculture faculty. No student had their own transport so we generally grouped together after breakfast for our walk to classes and back for lunch as well. An afternoon teatime was a regular in our Student Lounge but we would generally not walk back from the faculty for tea. Most times we would also be late coming back for dinner. Some of us eventually built special relationships with the servers in the residence dining hall, especially with Atia, to ensure they kept our selections for dinner warm until we came back. Weekends were spent studying, lounging in the hall around the swimming pool, sipping pineapple juice, and having a good time.

At that time University education was provided free by the government of Ghana for all students. Additionally, at the beginning of each semester all students were provided with an allowance for books and other school necessities. For the boys, the allowance was a wonderful opportunity to head into town to buy radios and speakers for their rooms and to have the means to take their girlfriends out to dinner and to the clubs. The ladies would generally hit the shops to buy the latest fashions from Kingsway and GNTC stores and essential accessories to dress up for classes.

Emelia at age 20

Afternoon "jumps," which were dances organized in clubs on weekend afternoons at Hotel de Kingsway, were a popular activity for Saturday outings with friends. Another highlight was the chilling at the coffee shop near the campus. Within ten days of receiving the allowance we would all be back focusing on our studies since we would have squandered all our money by then. Those were the good times. We studied hard but played hard as well.

CHAPTER 12

At the national level changes were brewing. General Ignatius Kutu Acheampong was the military head of state from 13 January 1972 to 5 July 1978. He was ruthless, seizing the assets of individuals and giving the military unparalleled authority in the country. A University of Ghana, Legon, student witnessed soldiers beating an unarmed man for a misdemeanor on the streets of Accra. He intervened and requested that they stop. The student was attacked by the military, stripped naked, and beaten till he could no longer walk. It was horrendous.

Back at the university, he informed the Student Representative Council (SRC). On seeing his bloodied body, they called for agitation by students and demonstrations against these ongoing atrocities. SRC leaders from Legon visited all the campuses and called for urgent staff meetings to brief students of what had transpired in Accra. We at Tech quickly mobilized and gathered outside on the grounds of the Great Hall, chanting and screaming after hearing hints of what had transpired in Accra.

We were stunned when we heard the details during the briefing. "How dare these half-educated, military men beat a young student for no just cause!" We were all furious the more we heard.

It did not take much for students from all three campuses—Legon, Cape Coast, and KNUST—to agree to join the upcoming national demonstrations against General Acheampong's military government on the upcoming Friday and march to the respective regional directors' offices.

There was singing and lots of noise on campus in anticipation of the demonstrations. It was a sleepless night for most of us. If a student in a university can be beaten on the side of the street for stopping an injustice he had witnessed, we could each of us be facing that same scenario down the road. We had to act, and we had to act in unison. We did not pause to think what would happen to any of us. We all agreed that we had to stop this brutality before it became the norm.

That Friday morning we quickly dressed up, wearing our campus t-shirts, and started getting ready to meet in front of the GNTC shopping centre where we were scheduled to start the march.

Just about 8:00 a.m. we heard the sounds of several large vehicles moving on campus. My women's hall, Africa Hall, was near the entrance of the campus, and we saw long fleets of military vehicles driving to our hall and others driving quickly past us and in the direction of both Unity and Republic Halls and beyond.

"What could this be?" we asked each other. We were scared but could not be deterred. We got ready and quickly went downstairs to meet the others in front of our Hall to gather and go together to the college meeting place.

Six or seven military vehicles were parked in front of Africa Hall loaded with military men in their uniforms. They stared angrily at us, batons in hand, as we walked right past them, defiant, in our

Emelia and her mother at home in Suame

large numbers to the junction of Africa and Okodie Roads.

We could see other students emerging from the Halls nearby and also starting to move to join us on our way. We felt emboldened and knew we were doing the right thing. After all, there was always safety in numbers.

Once we made the bend in the road toward the GNTC meeting point, having now been joined by a lot of the young men from the other student halls, the singing started. Just as the crowds began to gather, we heard some screams from behind. The military men that had now dispersed in their vehicles across the campus had jumped out of their vehicles and started beating whoever they could get their hands on.

People screamed and ran in different directions. I was terrified and started running toward the arts building in the direction of the other university exit. I could see when I turned to look behind that they had gotten ahold of my friend Felicia, and two men were repeatedly beating her with their batons. There was nothing I could do. I kept running. People were running everywhere and hiding wherever they could, behind bushes and in classrooms and offices close by. It was mayhem.

The military apparently had a coordinated plan across all the campuses, a plan to storm the campuses and beat the students to surrender. We were barely able to get out of the campus to start the demonstrations when the rampage started. The campus was in a state of utter chaos. The soldiers continued to beat whomever they could get their hands on. I finally was able to run and hide in the Tech Primary School where the young students were scared to see all of us rushing in all different directions. This craziness went on for most of the day. By early evening there was the beginning of some calm with the campus completely overtaken by the military. Some of us eventually managed to get out of the campus to the village across from the University, Ayigya. I took a taxi home with a number of my friends. We had no money, nothing, and had starved all day.

By the time we got home Maa was ready to die of anguish, having heard about the chaos on campus and unable to reach me. She embraced all of us with tears in her eyes and ours, not knowing where to start as we shared what had happened that day. We calmly settled down, had our showers, and had something to eat. Some of my friends stayed with us for a couple of days before heading on to their respective homes outside Kumasi when we realized we would be kept home for a while. We found out later that the military had planned all along to prevent us from our peaceful demonstrations, by storming all three campuses and beating the students at will with their batons. The government subsequently called for the closure of the universities to quelch any further demonstrations.

I spent a month at home hanging out with friends and on Sundays helping Auntie Akua and the team to knead the bread dough from the huge mill in the house. We sat all afternoon, hand kneading and rolling the dough into the greased baking pans to rise. Mondays were very busy as the bulk of the Turkson's Bakery bread supply to Kingsway and GNTC stores were done on Mondays. You would smell the early morning waft of baking bread in the morning from dawn. Those were a few of the times you planned to wake up early to get some freshly baked bread for breakfast. It literally melted in your mouth.

We had received notice that the university was to be reopened. I was eager to get back. The first week at home had been exciting but as the days and weeks rolled along there was great unease as to when the government would allow classes to resume, and I welcomed the news of the school's reopening. On that last Sunday working on the bread, the persistent rumbling I felt in my tummy was not the usual pains I had as my monthly period was about to begin. I complained to the ladies, and they teased me about perhaps looking for an excuse not to go back to school.

I moped around as best as I could until my ride came to take me back to school. I felt unwell but was not sure what the problem was. I went straight to bed when I got back to school that afternoon and stayed there. I woke up very early the next day, hoping to have an early start for my lectures. I could barely move my feet. I slowly stumbled, shaking, to the bathroom where I collapsed on the bathroom floor. Luckily, Theresa Amoah and Regina also had gotten up early. They entered the group bathroom to find me sobbing softly with my hands on my tummy on the fourth-floor bathroom.

One of them stayed with me while the other ran outside to call the housemistress and to get help. I was in pain. It must have been my lucky day. As it turned out Dr. Osafo had just parked his car in front of Africa Hall for a meeting with the housemistress. They helped me down the long flight of stairs downstairs into his car and took me to the University Hospital, a short ride away. I was immediately examined since it had not yet gotten busy in the morning. Dr. Gyapong, the doctor on call, assessed my situation and prescribed chloramphenicol, an antibiotic apparently very effective for infections. Regina called my mom who was suddenly sitting by my bedside by the time I woke up from a long sleep. Being a trained midwife, she was at ease in the hospital and pretty soon was chatting and making acquaintances there.

By Wednesday I could barely stand up straight. I was in a daze, in terrible pain in my abdomen, and now everyone around was getting worried. Why was the antibiotic not working? My friends and other classmates would stop by in the course of the day to sit with me and visit. I could no longer even carry on a conversation. Word spread in the Agriculture faculty and elsewhere that I was gravely sick. The evening came and passed with no progress.

Thursday evening came. Dr. Baafour-Senkyire from my faculty visited. He came with another doctor, Dr. Opoku. They spent some time examining me and talking to the nurses in the ward. In the end, he suggested I needed to be transferred to the main central hospital in Kumasi, Okomfo Anokye Hospital. I do not remember how I got to Okomfo Anokye. All I remember was a lot of buzz around me. Early the next morning I was wheeled into the operating theater for surgery. It was not until a couple of days later that I could then feel only the pain of the surgery and not the intense abdominal pain I had endured. I had apparently had a ruptured appendix. The chloramphenicol treatment had done nothing for it and had led to the abdominal cavity getting infected and becoming peritonitis, a potentially fatal infection if not treated immediately. I was very lucky, thanks to Dr. Opoku.

In the C ward where I was on the mend, there were other patients who were also suffering from peritonitis. Two middle-aged women on the ward had apparently also developed peritonitis after using variations of local herbs for enemas. That apparently was a common practice. I did not know. These women would cry in pain all night, and I wondered about the kind of care being provided. *Had every level of care been provided to them*? I wondered, even though deep down I felt I already knew the answer. My mind drifted to my missed ambition to become a doctor, but I found a way to slowly move my mind from that disturbing thought. Both women died. I vowed to remember chloramphenicol, the two women, and the two doctors for the rest of my life.

***

Maa took me back home to recuperate. That first evening she prepared a delicious vegetable soup with fish and mashed yam to welcome me safely back home.

When I returned to school after my hospitalization and surgery, there was a lot of concern about my welfare from the other students and faculty, those I knew and others I did not. Among the senior students in our department, Cudjoe Tsegah stood out in checking on me. For snacks, there were these two ladies who would sell roasted plantains under the neem trees between the Faculty of Agriculture building and the Social Sciences Department. As this had always been my favorite midday snack, I would periodically stop by the women to pick up some roasted plantains and peanuts. Cudjoe apparently noticed. We were suddenly meeting around the same time by the plantain sellers and would chat on our way back to our building. Over time we grew close, and before long we started dating.

There were a few other guys who were interested in dating me, but Cudjoe stood out. He was caring and pleasant to spend time with. We spent a lot of time together, taking long walks around campus or just relaxing on the benches in the park near Africa Hall, watching the traffic roll by. We would venture to Suame sometimes for some of Maa's great home cooking on weekends or to Opoku Ware Secondary School, where sister Rosebay was the domestic bursar at the time, for her great baking spoils and to bring food back to campus. Sister Rosebay was the second daughter of Auntie Mamaa, and it as always great to spend time with her and enjoy her cooking and to babysit her baby son, Abeeku. On holidays when I went to Accra to stay with Edith, Cudjoe and I would spend time together at his mother's shop at the Makola market and watch movies at Orion or Regal cinemas. We were definitely going steady, but it was not to last.

Before the end of my final year, the rumor mill started churning. A number of our mates had been to visit other friends at Cape Coast University and came back with word that they had met Cudjoe at Cape Coast visiting another girlfriend. I did not believe it at first. It could not be possible. Apparently, they had been whispering among other colleagues and friends but I was not aware of it for a couple of weeks. As the saying goes, "you are always the last to hear especially if the matter is of direct concern for you."

In my mind I had found a soulmate in Cudjoe so I was devastated. I avoided him when I saw him under the neem trees; I refused to talk to him for days. I moaned and lamented my loss and wondered what I could have done wrong for him to look elsewhere. When we finally sat down to talk about the situation, he apologized profusely and informed me it was nothing serious. This other lady, Abena, had been someone he knew before and had not meant for it to develop into anything. There was no good reason I could see for him visiting her at Cape Coast. We continued sporadically seeing each other but the trust was gone.

CHAPTER 13

During my study period at Wesley Girls and also at KNUST I was extremely lucky and exceedingly grateful for other external opportunities I received. During the first semester of Form 4, there was a competition for our grade students to submit applications for a summer abroad program in the United States. Quite a few of my friends and classmates sent in our submissions, not knowing whether anything would materialize. There had been similar opportunities for years but nothing happened. We all saw a trip to the United States as a lifelong dream, perhaps when one was working in the government sector. We knew there were study abroad programs during one's work life. Since opportunities during secondary school years were extremely limited, we all decided to take the chance and submit our extensive essays, just in case. This was supposed to be an individual assignment so we did not receive any support from our teachers, not that we did not try to ask them for help. Our teachers who were coordinating the submissions ensured we all submitted our applications on time and reminded us not to dream too much in case it did not work out.

Luckily for me, at the end of one study period I was called to our headmistress Ms. Garnett's office. You never want to be called to her office even though she was a warm, loving lady. This time, though, I was met with the good news that I had been selected for the summer abroad program. I jumped and hugged her for joy. Wow, what luck! She handed me the packet she had just received with the program details to review and submit all the additional information requested for planning my travel in a timely fashion. As was her generous and warm nature, she asked me to get back to the office the next day for me to call my mom to share the good news, which I did. Mom was elated. She was on cloud nine and I could imagine her jumping for joy just as I had done the day before. She would immediately start organizing, making new clothes for my travel, and putting together local Ghanaian presents for my American hosts.

This was the Experiment in International Living program based in Vermont, which sponsors young students from overseas to stay with families in the United States in the summer. As I learned later, this was a charitable organization supported by communities throughout the country. I was to be sponsored by the Rotary Club of Jerseyville, Illinois, with Bill and Jill Wieland as my primary hosts. Bill was the Headmaster of the Jerseyville Elementary School, and Jill volunteered extensively in the community. They had been foster parents for years and had adopted two children of their own, Danny and Martha.

I had no idea what my stay in the United States would be like. It was just sheer excitement on all fronts. I was going to get on a plane for the first time in my life and go to a faraway land by myself. To say I was both scared and excited was an understatement. Jerseyville, as it turned out, was a small rural community in Southern Illinois. It was only a couple of miles across the Mississippi River from St. Louis, Missouri. My stay was supported by six Rotarian families in the area, and I therefore spent time with each of the families during my stay. A couple of them were farmers, and one family worked as professors at nearby Principia College. I was a celebrity that summer. Everyone in town wanted to spend time with me. I had a wonderful time. Through presentations I made to the Rotary Club, meetings with students at Bill's school, and with others in Principia and nearby Alton, I was immersed in the community.

I learned about American agriculture and how milking was done, how the pigs were raised, and how the grain was stored in huge silos over winters. I was introduced to baseball through a couple of Cardinal baseball games in St. Louis. Baseball looked very similar to a game we had in Ghana called Rounders. That, however, was a girls' game. I was so fascinated to see men playing the game and astounded by the sheer numbers of people in the stadium watching them. Jill took me on a ride on the steel Gateway Arch. How could one build something like this? There was so much to learn everywhere I looked.

Bill and Jill's son Danny worked with the airline Trans World Airlines (TWA) at the time and lived in Joliet. We got the chance to see him and other family members in the area during my stay. Martha, however, was with the army and based in Fort Worth, Texas. Bill and Jill decided we should take a trip down south before I left to go back to school. I can still remember the rolling hills and greenery as we drove through Arkansas. Although I do not remember much of the trip, I remember being awed by the interstate network, the amenities accessible and available everywhere we went. Martha and I were similar in age, and we spent most of our time together learning about each other and sharing information about our very different cultures. I suddenly had a sister. It was wonderful although the time was short.

Every good thing had to come to an end. The summer breezed by, and before long I was to leave to go back to school. Goodbyes are never easy, and I had no idea if and when our paths would cross again. I had been warmly and intimately welcomed into the homes and lives of total strangers. I felt just as loved and appreciated as I was by my own folks in Suame. I knew these would be lifelong relationships because we all resolved to stay in touch with correspondence, which we do to this day.

A second opportunity came up during my third year at Tech for students of the agriculture faculty to apply for a Vacation Training Research Program at the International Institute of Tropical Agriculture (IITA) based in Ibadan, Nigeria. I saw the notice on our Faculty Bulletin Board and applied for it, then asked my classmate and good friend, Ohenese Apau Sakyi, to also apply. IITA was part of the global Consultative Group of International Agriculture Research (CGIAR) centers. Both Sakyi and I were selected to spend the summer of 1975 at IITA. What an opportunity. I had already decided to focus my final year specializing in crop science working under Dr. Dan Osafo so it provided an excellent opportunity to start my research work during my stay in Ibadan. IITA was an oasis of opulence and organization surrounded by the underdevelopment and poverty in the neighboring communities. All the facilities and infrastructure were set up as any institution in the developed world. It felt like being in the United States or elsewhere in the developed world.

***

My supervisor, Dr. Chris Wein, was patient and very knowledgeable. He introduced me to his research on cowpeas, and I spent my stay supporting him in his laboratory and greenhouses taking samples, analyzing his data, and assisting in report writing as needed. Sakyi and I were lucky to meet two Ghanaian scientists at the Institute, Dr. Seth Danso and Dr. Aba Ayanaba. They took us under their wings and would take us into town to the Ibadan market and on tours to the world-class University of Ibadan on weekends. We explored the neighboring towns of Ilorin and Abeokuta to learn their history and arts and mingle with the people in the bustling markets. The gossip at the Institute was that you could find any human part for sale in the Ibadan market. We steered clear of that section of the market.

Emelia and her mother at her graduation from KNUST

Our best times were during the social outings for the parties we were invited to by some of Dr. Danso's friends on weekends. These parties were always held in such elegant homes with the music pulsating through the entire neighborhood. The food spread could literally feed the entire town. The best of it, though, was that the host and hostess would change their elaborate outfits at least six or seven times in the course of an evening, with each outfit building on the previous one. Each of the men was referred to as *Oga* or *Oga phataphata,* indicating their rank in the society. We realized how important rank was to the community, and you always had to make sure you referred to people with their titles if you wanted to stay in their good books. Why was rank and constant mentioning of credentials so important? We did not know or understand at the time.

We left for Ghana with Sakyi having spent most of his allowance on a huge boombox to display to his friends back at Tech and with me having shopped for a suitcase full of beautiful fabrics to share with Maa and the rest of the family.

***

On our return from Ibadan, I focused my energy on completing my research on enhancing the yield of cowpeas growth and development in semi-arid conditions, having had the privilege of getting it started during the summer. Under the guidance of Dr. Osafo, I expedited the necessary literature review and mobilized needed support to get the field work completed and started to write my research dissertation. The final fourth year was when each student focused on their specialized area so the groups were much smaller for our lecturers. For crop science there were a total of six students. At the same time as we worked to complete our thesis, we formed study groups to review for the final exams, which we completed in May 1976. Not long after that our results came out. I was the top student in the class graduating with a First-Class Honors degree.

I was elated. I knew I had worked extremely hard throughout and was happy to be back on top like I had been at Wesley Girls.

I still wondered and struggled to understand why I did not do well on the A-Level examinations in the first place. I was slowly beginning to realize that life can definitely throw you some rough curves. I was beginning to learn to be open to whatever came my way and to always seek and explore other opportunities. This was not an easy path but, after my saga with medical school, I was now extremely content with where I was and how my life was shaping up. Although this was not what I had initially envisaged for myself, I had no regrets. I was moving forward.

The entire class had a group graduation party immediately after our graduation ceremony and prior to parting ways to start our one-year National Service Program. Maa brought us whole baskets of homemade cakes and cookies as well as our favorite jollof rice and chicken stew, enough to feed the entire class for our celebrations. Back at home we followed it up with a thanksgiving service at the home church of Kumasi Central Methodist, followed again with celebrations with family and friends at home. Maa was in her element.

CHAPTER 14

For National Service, I had a placement to teach biology at the Winneba Secondary School in Winneba in the Central Region. Winneba was the main town for the Efutu ethnic group, a renowned fishing town hosting one of the country's premier home science centers. It is situated between Accra and Cape Coast with ready access to both.

This was my first paying position with a monthly stipend of one hundred and fifteen Ghana cedis (GHs115 = $30/month in 1976). I shared a two-bedroom apartment with Sabina Wilson who had also graduated from Tech with a degree in the social sciences. Although we had not been close friends at Tech, we bonded very well together and were inseparable.

The country was still under military government, and life was beginning to get very difficult for most families. The GNTC and Kingsway shops had empty shelves. Whatever could be found was triple the previous price. Sometimes it was even difficult to find a loaf of bread to buy in the whole of Winneba town. Fortunately, one of the teachers was related to the new GNTC manager. Thus, at the beginning of the month when his supplies came in, there was a portion that was allocated to the teachers of the secondary school and the Home Science Training center. We would then plan a weekend trip to Swedru, a neighboring farming community, to purchase all our necessary produce.

In Swedru on market weekends, farmers from all the neighboring villages would bring their freshly harvested fruits and vegetables to the market. The farmers had no storage facilities for any of their harvests so it was imperative that they sell whatever they harvested during the week. Brokers from the larger cities such as Cape Coast and Accra would bring their big trucks to buy from the markets at a much lower cost and haul everything back to main markets in the big cities to sell. It was great business. Being close, we would get a ride and purchase all we needed at a much more reasonable price.

Winneba was a coastal town, and we relished the abundant seafood. Fishermen were not allowed to go out on Tuesdays. According to tradition, that was the day that the sea goddess and her children rested and did not want to be disturbed. It was a bad omen to go fishing on that day for fear of upsetting the gods who invariably, it was believed, would reduce the catch for the rest of the year.

In spite of the Tuesday ban, we had fresh fish every other day for our soups, stews, and the traditional *Fanti-Fanti*. This is a classic fish dish for which you put the fish, tomato, onion, pepper, and other spices, such as ginger, black pepper, and basil, and oil together and let it simmer slowly until everything is fully cooked. It was a quick meal for the fisherfolk when they returned from the sea at the end of the day. You would simmer it slowly while they bathed and freshened up. Then they ate the meal with rice or the traditional fermented corn dish, *kenkey*.

***

Relationships are never as straightforward as one might expect. You have to let them roll by in their own unique way. After our meeting in Accra when I was schooling in Cape Coast, Albert Timpo visited me occasionally during my preliminary year. After a couple of months of phone calls and his visits to Cape Coast, we started dating. On holidays when I went back to stay at my cousin Edith's place in Kaneshie, Accra, we would periodically go out for dinner or afternoon jump dances at Ringway or Ambassador Hotel. It was loads of fun.

I was beginning to think we were getting serious until one day I went with friends to the GNTC store near Makola market in downtown Accra. The heat was intense, and we had picked up a few items so we stood on the side of the road to get a taxi. All the taxis passing were full, and we were beginning to get overwhelmed. Luckily, as I turned toward the High Street stretching my neck to see if another taxi was around the corner, I saw the white Toyota Corolla, license plate GL161.

It had to be Albert. I knew the car, and I knew the number. I urgently flagged him down. I must have caught his eye. Wonderful. He slowed down and came to a stop right where we stood. We all said hello with big smiles on our faces. I asked if we could get a ride back home. I gave him a pleading look. There was no one with him. He apologized and said he was on his way somewhere else and could not deviate. We said thanks, and I knew everything was over. What gentleman will not give a ride to his girlfriend who so desperately needs one? "This relationship," I thought to myself, "is not going anywhere."

He later called to explain his rush that afternoon and apologized. I was still not convinced that we would continue dating. We saw each other a couple of times after that. He knew I was not happy about the ride, and he continued to assure me that he was serious about our relationship. Albert had studied medicine at the Hadassah Medical School in Israel with three other friends from Achimota. Dr. Kwaku Wuaku was practicing at the Akosombo Hospital. Both Dr. Hector Addo and Dr. Timothy Nutsugah were both at the Korle Bu Teaching Hospital. Another close friend of his, Dr. Abraham Harid, who was originally from Zimbabwe but also studied in Hadassah, was then in Ghana and working in Akuse Hospital, eighty kilometers outside Accra.

For weeks after "ridegate" Albert would pick me up for outings with his friends and their girlfriends. On evenings when they were not on call, we would all meet at one of the nice bar/dinner stops in Accra for dinner and drinks. They would spend so much time reminiscing about their days in Israel that the ladies would end up rolling our eyes and laughing them off. We even went one weekend to Akuse to spend the day with Abraham to have lunch and explore its environs. I was appeased.

During my studies at Tech, Albert and I continued to see each other periodically. His older half-brother, William Timpo, was on the Architecture faculty at Tech. William's wife, Gladys, was on the Agriculture faculty teaching horticulture and was also the Housemistress for Africa Hall residence where I was. On his first visit to Kumasi, he introduced me to his brother and family. Since I saw Mrs. Timpo often, both in class and in the hall of residence, we became very close. She started giving me and my friends rides back to the residence when convenient, sparing us the thirty-minute walk. She would take me out shopping when she went into town. Pretty soon she started buying her bread for herself and for other friends from Maa's bakery.

Just when I thought we were getting serious in our relationship, Albert informed me that he had received admission to do his Pediatric Residency at Lincoln Hospital in New York City and was to leave within months. That was a big surprise. He had briefly mentioned that he would be looking into the possibilities of going out of the country for further studies but I had not realized it was so soon. Apparently, it was not so easy to get ready admissions into residency programs. Additionally, communications and the mail delayed his receipt of the final admission details. He had received another admission to the University of Saskatchewan in Canada but opted for the New York City program due to the cold Canadian winters. He had experienced the cold in Israel and was not looking forward to more. I had no clue what the difference was. The hot weather always worked for me. I had no hand in his decisions, but I knew and understood that it was important for his career. I only wished him luck. Before long he left, with both of us promising to write often to each other and stay in touch.

Even before he left, I was already expecting his letters. Reality soon set in. I assured myself that he would need time to settle down in his new environment before writing and perhaps the program was already getting too demanding for him to have time for correspondence. After six months of waiting, I decided I had been forgotten on the other side of the Atlantic. It was time to move on.

CHAPTER 15

The National Service year was always a transition period that enabled young graduates to further assess and develop a roadmap for the future. It had been clear from Tech that I was interested in becoming a plant physiologist. Based on information gleaned from faculty members from Tech and other colleagues, Ghana at the time had two international plant physiologists managing the projects at the West African Cocoa Research Institute (WACRI) based at Tafo-Akim in the Eastern Region of Ghana. There was no Ghanaian plant physiologist. My good friend George Ofori-Koranteng grew up at WACRI, where his father worked, and we both talked a lot and dreamt of working there together in senior positions after we had our advanced degrees.

For my National Service year, I was assigned to Winneba Secondary School in the Central Region to teach high school biology. It was my first real job apart from summer temporary jobs at the College Farms at Tech and the National Lotteries one summer holidays. I was disappointed that I was not placed in a bigger city. However, Winneba was only thirty-five miles from Accra, and Cape Coast was fifty-five miles away so it was centrally located for me to visit friends over the weekend in both cities.

The teaching job was easy and uneventful. The students were eager to learn and enthusiastic. They would keep you in class long after the lecture was over with their questions, both related to the course and about life in general. They had aspirations of working hard and getting the opportunity to enter universities when the time came. I shared my experiences and repeatedly encouraged them to do their best all the time. Life has a way of throwing curves at you but with the right education, hopefully, it would always be easier to negotiate the turns.

Most of the teachers were supportive. The environment was different from Wesley Girls, though. Most of the students were from Winneba and the surrounding communities. There were a handful from other parts of the country but it was not as diverse as Wesley Girls. All the teachers were Ghanaian. The school was not as endowed with facilities; labs were not as fully equipped, and the sports facilities were limited. Although it was the only secondary school in Winneba, efforts were made, however infrequent, to have athletic and other programs with Apam Secondary School, which was barely half an hour away. In spite of this, the dedication and support of the teachers was very much the same. Students were expected and encouraged to excel. They were also given emotional support when they needed it.

Some of the students would volunteer to help us in our homes, as needed. I had moved to Winneba with Cynthia Opoku, the older daughter of my adopted sister Ama Obenewa from Suame. Cynthia had then completed her middle school Form 4 and was in transition on her next steps. As was the tradition in Ghana, when you settled down after graduation, parents would always ensure you are sent off with an extra hand to help in your new home.

In the same way as Sister Ama was sent from Kejetia to stay with Maa at Suame when she finished her midwifery course, Cynthia came to stay with me. She was considering setting up a catering business but had not yet decided. Winneba, with the Home Science Centre close by, provided an opportunity for her to interact with some of the students and to determine if that was the path for her. A number of my colleagues had friends teaching at the Home Science Institute so introductions and arrangements were made for Cynthia to sit in a number of classes during the year we were together at Winneba.

Our stay in Winneba was short but we had a wonderful time. The new relationships were lifelong and provided an excellent springboard to living away from family. Once I was settled in at Winneba, I started exploring opportunities in the United States and elsewhere for further studies. Most of our faculty at Tech had either studied for their post-baccalaureate degrees in the United Kingdom or Australia; that's where the options were in addition to Eastern Europe during their time. More opportunities were now opening up in the United States through new scholarships being offered by the Ghana Scholarships Secretariat.

The Secretariat was established under the office of the president in 1960 and mandated to handle and award government scholarships for human resource development and growth of the country. It was set up to provide an open system to support the expansion of academic opportunities to students across the country with a strong focus on competence and no regional biases. In reality, as with most such endeavors, nepotism was prevalent, and you always needed someone with connections to someone else to access opportunities that should be available to all.

I decided to take my chances on this one. Dr. Osafo, my advisor at Tech, had suggested focusing on the land grant colleges in the United States since they are all renowned for their agricultural programs. I applied to only two colleges since the application fees, postage costs, and other expenses were high. I did not want to ask Maa for money unless I really needed to. Since I had already visited Illinois and loved the place and the people, I applied to the University of Illinois in Urbana-Champaign, in addition to Cornell University in Ithaca, New York. My anticipation grew over the months, and before long, to my great joy, I received admission to both Cornell and the University of Illinois and also received the necessary scholarship through the Ghana Scholarship Secretariat. I could not contain my joy.

Maa again was in her element on hearing the news. My colleagues at Winneba were so excited for me they organized an impromptu party to celebrate the good news. Sabina had a boyfriend who was already in the United States. They were getting ready to be married so she was preparing to join him after the National Service. We started making plans about how we would see each other in the States so we could spend time together and explore the country. By that time I had learned Urbana-Champaign was much colder than Ithaca so I decided to accept the offer from Cornell. Besides, it was the college where my advisor in Ibadan, Dr. Chris Wein, had attended and had been on the faculty. It had to be good.

Long gone were the days when I could not get admission to the Ghana Medical School. I was now on a very different path, and the pieces appeared to be falling in place. I kept focused and traveled several times to Accra to the Ghana Scholarship Secretariat to follow up on my application now that I had admissions in hand. My persistence paid off, and late in July 1977 I received all the necessary documentation on financing and flight tickets. On receipt of my admission documents for Cornell, I wrote to Albert to let him know I would be coming to New York. I had not heard from him in a very long time but decided to write anyway. To my surprise he responded immediately and promised to meet me on arrival in New York City. I was elated.

On 14 August 1977, I set off on a new journey in pursuit of education and experiences that would bring me back to Ghana as the first female plant physiologist. On the flight from Accra to John F. Kennedy (JFK) airport were Michael Simpson and other colleagues from Tech who had also received scholarships for further studies in other parts of the United States. We all parted ways at the JFK airport for our different destinations.

Albert was at the airport to meet me on arrival. In truth, I was not sure he would be there so I was pleasantly surprised. From the JFK airport to his apartment in the Parkchester section of the Bronx, I could only focus on the road. We took the Whitestone Bridge. It must have been four lanes in each direction with so many cars. The highway had more overpasses and exits and turns than I could count. I was awed and wondered how people could navigate their way in this maze of roads. I did not recall seeing such roads when I was in Jerseyville with the Wielands.

This was now the real America we had dreamt about and seen in movies. My stomach was churning with excitement. Albert's apartment complex was a huge maze with parks and gardens. We passed several shopping areas off the Grand Concourse as we headed to the apartment, a cozy one-bedroom. I was exhausted from the trip but we stayed up late as he gave me all the details of his new life in New York City. It sounded fascinating, and I suddenly understood why he never seemed to have the time to write.

I was in the city for only two nights, then Albert drove me to the Port Authority with its maze of buses and people all moving as if orchestrated to music. Buses were scheduled to head all over the country. I was amazed at the organization of the place, with shops everywhere you looked. My mind was thrown back to the Kejetia Lorry Station in Kumasi where I would start my Cape Coast trips for years. It is a very different world I was entering.

My Greyhound bus was on the fourth floor of the Port Authority. Through escalators and lifts we arrived at the gate and waited for the bus to depart. With tears in my eyes, I waved at Albert standing at the gate. He promised to visit me in Ithaca when he had a break in his schedule. On that sunny August morning, we headed north on the West Side Highway along the Hudson River toward the Tappan Zee Bridge, which would connect us with Route 17 to Binghamton where I would change for another bus enroute to Ithaca. As I watched the river sparkle in the sunlight, I wondered how the low-lying Tappan Zee Bridge could be so long.

CHAPTER 16

When I arrived in Ithaca on that beautiful sunny August day, the leaves were just beginning to hint at the autumn to come. The narrow roads from Binghamton were encased with sky high trees with leaves of all hues, nature's handiwork, and enveloping views of the beautiful Cayuga hills. I fell immediately in love.

Registration was in the Sage Hall, the ancient building at the center of the campus, which at the time also served as one of the graduate student dormitories. I had my room on the third floor. There was a students' lounge and a kitchen on the first floor where we could cook and socialize. The dorm had a mix of students from all over the country as well as other international students.

Since almost all the students in Sage Hall were new at Cornell, we asked the same questions: Where were the classrooms and cafeterias? Who are you? Where are you from, and what are you studying? We met for an orientation session across the street at the Willard Straight Hall. Within a day or two of my arrival, I met another Ghanaian, Akweley Annan, who had just arrived from Accra for graduate studies at the Home Ecology Department. We became fast friends. There were a couple of Sudanese students who became regulars in the kitchen with Akweley and me.

The orientation days gave us an excellent opportunity to wander the campus and admire the scenic surroundings and buildings spread out over the hills and through the valleys. I could easily see how much walking was going to be necessary to traverse this magnificent campus. I was ready. The first couple of days were pleasant and very sunny. As I was used to back home, I would wake up and look outside. Once I knew it was sunny, I knew exactly what to wear. The third day I went through the same routine and went out to quickly go to the bookshop just about a hundred yards from Sage. In spite of the glowing sun, I walked out and literally froze. It was very cold for someone used to ninety degrees Fahrenheit weather most of the year. I hurriedly went back to the dorm and spoke to one of my new colleagues I had met the day before who happened to be heading outside as well about how cold it was outside. He looked at me with a laugh. "Yes, Emelia, you will be cold, considering what you are wearing," he said.

I saw absolutely nothing wrong with what I was wearing. He was from Pennsylvania. He told me I had to listen to the weather announcement each day to know what the temperature was going to be and dress accordingly. Hmm, that was new. I went back to my room and put on one of the sweaters I had brought with me from Ghana, then headed back out. I still froze in that short walk. Lesson number one: I have to get to the shops and buy some appropriate clothes if I am to survive. I was told August was nothing to write home about in terms of cold. I had to prepare for the Ithaca winter. I started putting together my shopping list with a radio at the top of that long list.

Lectures began. I had been assigned Dr. Ralph Obendorf as my advisor. He had his laboratory on the sixth floor of the relatively new Bradfield Hall within the Agriculture Quadrangle on Campus. Ralph and the entire team in the laboratory received me with warmth and care. The two other graduate students were Tran, originally from Vietnam, and Michael, from New York. I spent quite a bit of time with Ralph at the beginning to get to know each other and for him to ensure I was comfortable in this very new learning environment. There was absolute support not only from my lab colleagues but from all the professors I had courses with or met occasionally in the corridors. The expansive Mann Library at the head of the agriculture quadrangle became my second home away from home. I would eventually get a couple of hours of work organizing the returned books on the shelves.

I brought to Cornell the same enthusiasm and zeal for learning, which had been ingrained in me from Wesley Girls. I reached out to the professors as needed when I wanted extra clarity on any subject matter. The availability of tutorial hours was a new concept to me, but I took full advantage of them for all my lectures, spending time with the teaching assistants and other course mates. I worked hard and excelled in all my classes except organic chemistry. That was a disaster.

Organic chemistry was an introductory course. Lectures were held in a huge auditorium in Baker Hall with over a thousand students filled up to the top of class, busily taking notes. There was barely any space to interact with the faculty. You also literally needed special glasses to see the lecturer if you sat anywhere at the back of the hall. While the tutorials helped to clarify the coursework, I found the whole experience so impersonal and not conducive to the learning I wanted or was used to. I completed the course with a passable C grade and was relieved to have it over and done with.

There were so many novel experiences for me at Cornell. The Big Red Barn was the main cafeteria close to my office so a group of us would go over for lunch from time to time. I loved the creamy mashed potatoes. Potatoes were novel enough, much softer than the yams, cocoyams, and the white sweet potatoes we had in Ghana. How can one add butter and milk to potatoes? It was all so foreign but I devoured it each time and longed for more. It literally melted in my mouth each time.

One Saturday afternoon in late November, a friend and I decided to take a walk around campus to while away the time and admire the beautiful scenery. Almost as soon as we walked out toward the mound across from the Campus Bookstore, I saw white flakes coming down from the skies. I screamed, "Is that what I think it is?" My very first sighting of snow!

It began to come down heavily. The little girl in me came out. I twirled around and tried to catch some of the snowflakes, which kept melting as soon as they touched my hand. It took me back to all the songs we had memorized and sung as children in the ninety-degree heat of Ghana. Now I was actually seeing the miraculous, beautiful snow fall. Yes, there really was a God that poured the rain and the snow onto earth to water the grass and the trees. I was mesmerized.

There was much more snow to come in Ithaca. At times it would snow for days nonstop. By the time February rolled along, we seemed to be constantly surrounded by snow. I had bought all the warmer clothes and boots I needed and savored the beauty all around me. Wearing boots was always a challenge; they felt so heavy on my feet. It took a lot of learning to comfortably move around in them. I can recall the numerous times I tripped and fell in the snow all the while admiring the beauty it brought to my life during those times. I can recall in May the next year, seeing the melting snow with tulips and crocuses peeking out around the snow mounds. Ithaca, along with the entire Finger Lakes region, was a complete haven of peace and tranquility, fostering learning and growth.

Cornell had a vibrant International Students Office, which catered to all the international students on all aspects of student life. The office became the place to meet and share with other students who were far away from home with no connections in the USA. They organized several events throughout the year and helped place students with families in Ithaca, especially during the Thanksgiving and Christmas holidays when most students were away from the campus. My first Thanksgiving dinner was organized by the International Students Office a week before Thanksgiving at the Willard Straight Hall. So much food and so much fun.

There was also a small Ghanaian community at Cornell, mostly graduate students pursuing Ph.D.s. In that group were Conrad Bonsi (plant pathology), Mohammed Chambas (political science), Emmanuel Mensah (education), and Emmanuel Atayi (agricultural education). Matilda Hesse (home economics) was the matriarch of our group, ensuring we got together often at her apartment to share stories and enjoy her delicious home cooking such as peanut soup and fufu, jollof rice and chicken stew or banku (fermented corn meal dish similar to kenkey but cooked completely and molded into balls without the plantain leaves) and okra stew. We became a tightly knit family. I found out about the Salvation Army store in downtown Ithaca, at the foot of the hill descending from College Town. It became my go-to place to buy good quality household kitchen items at giveaway prices.

Akweley and I pooled our resources to cook together. Going for our monthly shopping at the grocery store in College Town, we marveled at all the filled-up shelves with unfamiliar items. For cereal we always purchased Corn Flakes and Rice Krispies, which we knew in Ghana, but there were whole shelves with different kinds of cereals. We were determined to try everything in the different food categories. We never missed buying ice cream. It was a treat. We would load our cart to the brim and end up spending just about one hundred dollars per person for the month. We improvised with the Indian Head brand corn meal to make our Ghanaian kenkey or banku, which we enjoyed with fried fish and tomato gravy when we felt like having our own local food. Occasionally, someone would find plantains, which we would fry and have with black-eyed bean stew just like we used to have in Ghana.

One difficult part of life was communication with home. There were a number of communication centers in College Town where you could make international calls. You needed to book two weeks in advance, then be allocated a specific time to show up for the call. At the allotted time an operator would dial the call and transfer it to you in a different numbered cubicle. You literally had to scream to be heard. I cherished those times, nonetheless, because it was only then I could talk to Maa and give her updates of how I was doing. Although we did not get the chance to talk much on the

Emelia and family at Cornell University

phone, I kept in touch with Maa and the rest of the family through constant letter writing. I would buy monthly a pack of the prepaid, pre-folded, blue airletter cards from the post office and write letters to family and friends so we could keep abreast of each other's lives.

After a year in Sage Hall, Akweley and I decided to find an off-campus apartment to share. We moved to the Marvin apartments, a lovely townhouse complex close to the campus, College Town, and a shopping center, just across from the cemetery near us, about a fifteen-minute walk to the agriculture quadrangle where we had most of our lectures. It was a two-bedroom townhouse with a kitchen and living room and plenty of space to socialize.

We were drawn to Marvin because our Ghanaian friends lived there. It was a perfect place for us. Although we didn't have cars and the local bus routes weren't located nearby, Conrad and Emmanuel were always gracious and helpful in taking us shopping at the nearby shopping center and even to the Triphammer Mall, which was much farther away but had a lot more shops to browse and explore.

Albert and I stayed in touch, and I would visit with him in New York on weekends and long holidays. On some of his weekends off he would also come to visit Ithaca. We became a serious couple during the first year, and he was a regular part of the Ghanaian community in Ithaca. Once in New York we went on the Circle Line cruise around Manhattan, which provided an awesome perspective on the history and buildings in the city. Walks in Central Park were a regular weekend feature. Our Ghanaian community started to grow. Within the Parkchester complex where Albert stayed were a number of other Ghanaians. We became close friends with Sophia and Kingsley Orraca-Tetteh as well as Mary and Ben Brew. Sophia had been a year ahead of me at Wesley Girls, and we had both been in Waldron House. We reconnected, and it was a delight to spend time with them. They introduced Albert to a number of their other Ghanaian medical residents in our complex. They all knew each other as colleagues from the Ghana Medical School. But since Albert went to medical school in Israel, he did not know any of them. There were a number of them he recognized who had been at the same Achimota secondary school where he went.

CHAPTER 17

By the spring of 1978, I was pregnant. I was sick a lot of the time but kept up with my lectures and my lab work. It was not easy. Not so much because of the college work but I was suddenly so worried about being pregnant but not married. I did not know what to do. Albert didn't say anything, and I was not going to bring up the subject. I called Maa several times and would wail the entire time on the phone. Maa in her usual loving way assured me that it was okay to have a child and not be married. The important thing was to take good care of myself so I could have a healthy baby; she would help in whatever way she could.

I could not be consoled. I recalled Maa talking to Matilda one weekend. In late April when Albert came to visit, Matilda invited us for lunch. In the course of our visit, she informed Albert that Maa had asked her to inquire directly from him if he had any intentions of marrying me or talking to my family. After a long discussion Albert assured her that he would talk to her and Maa in due course. I said nothing to Albert, leaving him to make his own decision. In my mind I was okay with being a single parent. That decision made the tears dry up, and I started making my own plans. I decided I needed to continue to grow as an independent person. Life had already thrown me some curves, and I had survived. This was another life decision I needed to be able to deal with as best as I could.

In late May Albert informed me he wanted us to get married. As the Ghanaian custom demanded, he would have his family at home go to make the necessary arrangements in Ghana. Although my dad had had very little to do with my life, the Ghanaian custom demanded that he be the one to make the decision and agree to our marriage. It was a very unfair practice but we had no say in the matter at that time. His older brother, George, and eldest sister, Adobea, with support from Maa, made the initial trip to Cape Coast to ascertain from Papa the date that his family could officially come and ask for my hand.

For Akan traditional marriages, it was important for the man's family to consult the head of the girl's family for the dowry and engagement list items to present to the girl's family when asking for their daughter's hand in marriage. It was very important to go with senior members of the family; otherwise, it would be perceived as being disrespectful.

The list of items to be presented also varied from family to family so it was important to ensure you received the list from the girl's family directly and not make any assumptions. In general, the list would include six pieces of traditional cloth for the bride, the dowry, some money, cloth and sandals for the bride-to-be's mother, similar items for the father, money for the brothers

Emelia and Albert
on their wedding day, 1978

referred to as *akontasikan*, a Bible, an engagement ring, suitcases with other gifts, utensils, jewelry, and food and drinks to entertain the family during the formal presentation. These items were topped with at least two bottles of the original green bottle Schnapps imported from Holland. A request for marriage is never complete without Schnapps.

A date was set for mid-May, and the list of what they needed to bring was agreed upon between the two families. We decided to get married in June. Albert never gave me a real explanation of why someone had to ask him if he was interested in marriage before he came forward. It did not sit well with me but I let it pass. Much later in life I wondered if indeed it was the best decision I made in not pressing for clearer insight behind his decisions. But sometimes situations get clearer in hindsight. At that point in time I was happy to go along.

The sky was clear and the weather was warm on our wedding day. It was an intimate lovely wedding. I was disappointed Maa was not going to be there for her only daughter's wedding. Matilda took charge as mom-in-chief. Albert's friend Abraham was now practicing at the Walter Reed Hospital in Washington, DC, so Albert asked him to be his best man. Akweley was my maid-of-honor. Bill and Jill Wieland flew in from Illinois. Other family friends—Regina from my Tech class, Ato Degraft-Johnson and Albert's brother Clement and cousin Samson—came in from Chicago. With all the Ghanaian community in Ithaca in attendance, decked out in our national colorful Kente cloth, as well as my office and some graduate school friends, we were all set.

The wedding was held at the Sage Chapel, the elegant and historic college church at the center of Cornell University. Sage Chapel, named after Henry Sage, a trustee at the school, was designed in 1872 by the Reverend Charles Babcock, the first Professor of Architecture at Cornell University, with stonework provided by a local stone-carver and several stained-glass windows made by Tiffany. The interior building has a rich and detailed history with many of the artistic renderings representing numerous Christian and educational themes. The music from the church was always mesmerizing, and you would hear the echoes from several of the buildings around. The organ incorporates pieces of previous organs. The building has several Tiffany glass and stained-glass windows.

Mr. Mensah walked me down the aisle, and the wedding was officiated by Reverend William Rogers who was the college chaplain at the ecumenical church I attended on campus. The wedding was followed up with a reception in the main hall of Anabel Taylor Hall. There was no honeymoon. That would come later, we agreed. Anabel Taylor Hall was a beautiful Gothic building with high-pitched roofs and served as a key building for spiritual and ecumenical activities on campus. It was just up the road from College Town with a view of Cornell's magnificent McGraw Clock.

I was scheduled to deliver at the end of August so had already started preparing for the arrival of our baby at the same time as we planned for the wedding. It was not to be. A week after the wedding I went into labor on a Friday night. Albert was already in New York. We called Conrad who came almost immediately to take me to the Tompkins County Hospital. My mind flew back to Suame and the numerous women I had seen in my lifetime coming to our home to deliver their babies at my mom's Turkson's Maternity Home. I remembered the endless screams in the middle of the night coming from the labor ward above our bedroom.

I was scared. I took consolation in having Conrad around for a while. The nurses at the hospital were extremely reassuring, rubbing my back as needed. It was in the middle of the night in a quiet hospital so they had all the time in the world for me. I calmed down a bit. My beautiful baby, Awoye Ama, was delivered prematurely very early that Saturday morning. Conrad had called Albert in the middle of the night, and by late that day he was in Ithaca to see his daughter. Awoye was named after Albert's aunt with whom he had spent most of his formative years in Peki-Dzake in the Volta region of Ghana. Ama is the Akan name for a girl born on Saturday. I was devastated not being able to bring Awoye home with me upon my discharge. For the next two weeks, I pumped my breast milk at home in the evening and brought it daily to the hospital to spend the day with Awo in the nursery until I was finally able to bring my new bundle of joy home with me to Marvin Lane.

Awoye and I spent the summer in New York City with Albert and came back in August for the second year of my program. We had made plans, and Maa was able to come from Ghana to spend the year with us in Ithaca to help take care of Awoye while I continued my college work without worrying about her care. It was perfect. Maa ended up knowing a lot of the families within our complex as she took Awoye daily in her stroller outside to get some fresh air. I knew it was a special privilege to have Maa spend the year with us. A number of other international students at the time also had their parents with them to help with the young children while they went to school. I appreciated every day with Maa as I could also see a lot of couples struggling with the complicated schedules of school and childcare and the related high costs of childcare with our meager student allowances and scholarships. With Maa around I was able to focus intently on my research and coursework.

***

My research on "in vitro culture of immature Soybean (Glycine Max) seeds and pods" was progressing, and my coursework was going very well. Getting both my research data analyzed and the thesis typed for clearance was another story. I would be found outside lecture periods on the ground floor of Uris Hall preparing my data punch cards to be submitted by the evening deadline to the computer lab. The computer lab hosted the entire computing center for the college. The process enabled all research data to be submitted with the punch cards. Then overnight the computer programmers would run the relevant programs and print out the long, folded green and white sheets of paper with all the tabulated results for collection the next day. One mistake in any data point resulted in the need to repunch all the data and resubmit for overnight processing.

I became a fixture in Uris Hall. Once I had my data summarized, I earnestly started my analysis and write-up. In the meantime, through Tran and Brian in my lab, I identified a typist who would type my thesis. Here again a change in any page once typed meant all subsequent pages had to be discarded and retyped since there was no way to insert new material and other edits and have the thesis maintain the formats required for submission.

Very few students owned typewriters at the time; even if they did they would not have the time or wherewithal to type other people's theses. The typing of the thesis was a long, prolonged saga but I was lucky and happy to have a competent typist to work with to get it done. With Maa around I focused intently on my research and coursework and was able to graduate with my master's degree in agronomy in May 1979 within the planned two-year period.

CHAPTER 18

You guessed it. I had already been looking at options for my Ph.D. Albert and I decided it would be better to live together than make the long commutes. If I was in college in New York City or New Jersey, Albert could still commute to work in the city as needed. I loved New York City whenever I was there but did not want to live there. I had fallen so much in love with Ithaca; I wanted a more suburban area. I knew there would not be another institution with the Cornell ambience but still wanted a more rural environment. We decided on Rutgers University in New Brunswick, New Jersey, and I got admission to start my Ph.D. in botany and plant physiology.

We had made lifelong friends in Ithaca but it was time to move on and settle down as a family. I knew I would miss Ithaca and everyone so much. At the end of the semester with graduation and my thesis submitted, there were a lot of tearful goodbyes to all my friends and colleagues. Albert came to pick us up, and we moved to New Jersey.

Rutgers was so different from Cornell. Cornell had a huge campus but it was all in the same place and one could easily walk anywhere around the campus. Rutgers, on the other hand, had five campuses spread out between New Brunswick and Piscataway. I was able to secure married students' accommodations on Busch Campus in Piscataway, although my laboratory and most of my lectures were at Cook College across the Raritan River in New Brunswick. I would make it work. As it turned out most of the students in our student housing were international students from Africa and elsewhere. A new Ghanaian community evolved out of our housing area as well as from the Rutgers/Livingston Day Care Centre where we enrolled Awoye. I was amazed at the large number of international students from all continents enrolled at Rutgers. It became a new and very enriching community for us. There was a sizable number of African families including Ghanaians, Nigerians, Ugandans, and several others from northern and southern Africa.

Maa departed to go back to Ghana after over a solid year with us. She had also made a lot of friends and acquaintances. Everyone in the new home in the Marvin neighborhood knew her. One could often hear her laughter from afar socializing in the children's playground with the neighbors. We were truly appreciative of her love and commitment to us and were sad to see her leave. It was not to be her last visit.

The three years for my doctoral program were extremely demanding both on the academic and personal fronts. On the academic end, the coursework was relatively easy, and I was coasting with straight As. The demands of my research work were a different matter. My advisor was Dr. Carlos Neyra. Originally from Peru, he was extremely demanding but very supportive and provided excellent guidance.

For the first couple of months, we had recurring issues with the temperature and moisture controls in the greenhouse. Our Polish lab assistant, an amiable and responsible helper, was often out sick and unavailable to provide the needed support. Once these problems were resolved, everything else went well. My laboratory mates were very different from my lab mates at Cornell. They had both worked with Dr. Neyra for years and were not in any great hurry to complete the program. I knew I could not afford to work in the lab forever since I still had my scholarship from the Ghana Scholarship Secretariat with strict timelines and expectations to maintain so I could receive financial aid.

I was getting a greater understanding of life in America. During her stay Maa had been introduced to soap operas, watching them in the afternoons with her new female friends at Marvin Lane. I would spend time watching a bit with her, especially during holidays and other days when I came back to the apartment for one thing or the other. Pretty soon I was completely hooked on *General Hospital, All My Children* and *One Life to Live.* On *General Hospital*, I could not help but follow closely the love life of *General Hospital*'s Luke and Laura, their plans to elope, and whatever other intrigue they were involved in. Following the twists and turns of Erica on *All My Children* became an addiction. I had to watch it myself because I kept telling Maa she was not giving me enough of the details on what was happening when I could not watch.

Before long, on days that I did not have lectures at the same time as the soap opera, I would find myself leaving my lab at the edge of Cook Campus to walk to the Student Center just across the street from the Douglas Campus to watch the shows. I was fascinated with the stories and the screen lives of the actors and actresses. Little did I realize that I was not the only one to get sucked into watching soap operas. Apparently, it was a popular national pastime.

I suddenly understood what one of my lab mates used to say about his mom and her friends who were spending most of the day staying home and watching soap operas. He lamented often about how frivolous their lives were. I would often argue with him and impress upon him the importance of holding our moms in high esteem. It was a lost cause with him. It was much later I came to realize that his mom and friends were from affluent families and could afford to stay home and enjoy the leisurely afternoons he often talked about.

***

Graduation from Rutgers University with a Ph.D.

By this time a few more of my Tech classmates had also arrived in the USA for further studies. Evelyn and Chris Opoku had settled in Houston, Araba and Kwamina Assabil were in Pittsburgh, Robert Otsina was in Iowa, and Kwabena Ampim was at Ohio State University. We all tried to stay in touch with each other. It appeared each time we reached out, we had news of other colleagues leaving Ghana for other countries to pursue higher education. We would all reminisce about our desire and plans to go back to Ghana on completion of our courses.

Meanwhile, everyone was working hard to complete the advanced degree programs as soon as we could.

The political situation in Ghana was unraveling with the new military government in power after the 1979 coup d'état led by Jerry John Rawlings, a flight lieutenant of the Ghana Air Force. With the coup and its uncertain aftermath, the Ghana mission in Washington, DC, which managed our scholarships, was unsure of the status of the scholarships so we had no assurance that they would not be canceled without notice. It was an uneasy time.

In the meantime I was pregnant with our second child, and Maa had already agreed she would come back to help us when the baby was born, but we could not be sure if she would be given a visa again. I would recall the numerous times my scholarship money was delayed for months at Cornell and scrambling to find on-campus work to be able to buy groceries. Those times I was lucky to find a couple of hours working at the Mann library. Now with one child and another on the way and up to my limits with my lab work, I was starting to feel a nagging anguish in my tummy.

Albert was still commuting from Piscataway to New York for work so extra help was urgently needed. We had been lucky to have Abena Ofori-Mensah, one of our new Ghanaian friends with a young child of her own, ready and available to help us with babysitting Awoye after Maa left. It had been very welcome since I had unpredictable schedules with my research work.

I realized again and again that I needed to slow down and carefully align my priorities with the realities of my situation. I had been in other tight situations, and I had to believe this would also get sorted out eventually. After repeated calls to the Ghana Education attaché in the Ghana Mission in Washington, DC, I was assured that there would be no change in my scholarship so long as I was maintaining the necessary grades and on course to complete on schedule. The Embassy had decided to no longer extend Ph.D. awards beyond their three-year limit. I was determined to soldier on.

My thoughts always go to my grandma, Maame Ama Atta, when I am in a bind. She would tell us that there was no road that was too hard to travel. You must find a way to go around it if you are unable to climb it. My mind was set. I worked hard to get Maa's visa application documents submitted. Abena agreed to continue babysitting Awoye and even my second child as needed. I pressed on. My daughter Emefa was born on 15 April. My delivery was delayed so the doctors decided to induce the labor on that day if I had not delivered by then. That morning Albert and I dropped off our tax return in the mailbox in front of St. Peter's Medical Center in New

Brunswick and went in to deliver our beautiful daughter with absolutely no complications. Maa had three boys, and I was making up for her with my two girls. Everyone was overjoyed. With Maa around and Abena to provide any necessary backup babysitting support, I was able to press on and completed my program at the end of three years.

CHAPTER 19

The attainment of one's dreams always comes with determination, and always at a cost. In the years that I had been studying in the States the political environment in Ghana had been rapidly deteriorating. Flight Lieutenant Jerry Rawlings staged two successful coup d'états, the first on 4 June 1979, holding onto power until 30 September 1979. Long-scheduled elections were held, and Rawlings handed over power to the People's National Party (PNP) government under President Hilla Limann. Limann served from 1979 to 1981 until the second coup d'état by Rawlings on 31 December 1981. Rawlings then hung on to power as the head of the Provisional National Defense Council (PNDC) until 1992 with the return to civilian rule.

In 1992 Rawlings transitioned to an elected President with his National Democratic Congress (NDC) party. The three-month period when Rawlings was in power, from June to September 1979, was a time of unspeakable atrocities against traders and businesspeople, both women and men. The PNDC period was no less traumatic for the people of Ghana. The new military government after the Jerry Rawlings coup of June 4, 1979, has over time brought Ghana to its knees.

The government had progressively enhanced its massive crackdown of people who they deemed to be affluent, whether the resources had been legitimately accrued or otherwise. Neighbors reported neighbors, and there was a general sense of fear and a premonition that the new government would seize property and money from individuals and companies. In this context, businessmen and women who would ordinarily order goods from abroad to sell or buy locally ceased operations. Shortages began to abound, and within a very short period of time the store shelves were empty. When coming to Ghana from overseas, it was common to fill suitcases with toilet paper, rice, oil, and other necessities for one's family. After the 1981 coup d'état, there was a massive exodus of Ghanaian professionals to Nigeria and other African countries. Some ventured as far away as Papua New Guinea, the Caribbean, and elsewhere. Those who could move to Europe or North America tried desperately to leave.

Albert and I had been looking forward to moving back home. I wanted to fulfill my dream of working as a plant physiologist at the Cocoa Research Institute. But now, Ghana was not a place that anyone would recommend. Family and friends encouraged us not to return. I had a chance to go to Ghana at the end of 1981 to represent Albert at his mom's funeral since he was unable to travel at the time. It was not the same place I had thoroughly enjoyed with my meager national service salary in Winneba, when all I needed was easily available. In 1981 even if you had the resources, you could not purchase goods, and there was no indication when the situation might be resolved. It was a very difficult decision for us to make at the time but we decided to remain in the States for a while until the situation at home improved. We had sent substantial amounts of money home to purchase a house, and suddenly all the plans were in limbo. We had to map out a new road.

During my studies I had been exposed to a number of agricultural research institutions where I could work in the States. Rutgers professors, especially a few of the faculty at Cook College, had been collaborating extensively with American Cyanamid and FMC in Princeton, New Jersey. Some had partnerships with Merck in Rahway, New Jersey, as well as with Dupont in Delaware. As I started researching opportunities around the area, I found there were a significant number of entry-level research positions I could apply for. I discussed options with my advisor and other faculty members who all encouraged me. I was lucky to have several interviews, especially at FMC and American Cyanamid within their plant research divisions.

I applied for several positions over a period of months. In most cases I would be contacted shortly after the submission of my application for interviews. There was always anticipation and excitement. After my first and sometimes second interviews I would hear back from the company to inform me that I was either overqualified for the position or did not have enough years of experience. The positions I was applying for were all entry-level Ph.D. positions, which had indicated lab research experience while pursuing my degree would be considered for years of experience. How was I to have relevant outside of college experience if I was not being given an opportunity with entry-level positions? Why were some companies indicating I was overqualified, and others felt I was underqualified? What was I missing? I was not going to be deterred. I would look further afield.

By this time Albert had been able to get a new position with the Rutgers Community Health Plan (RCHP) Group based in Princeton so he no longer had to commute to New York City. Not ready to give up, I applied to any position in line with my qualifications and experience. I spoke to colleagues and friends who urged me to keep trying. After almost a year of job-searching, one day while having lunch with some friends the issue of my eternal job search came up. One colleague suggested that I might not be getting any offers for positions because I was black and African. My jaw dropped.

It was as if someone had poured cold water on me. What was that supposed to mean? I knew I had been hearing on the news periodically that there were very few women in the sciences and that organizations were making an effort to change that situation. How did that apply to me? I had worked extremely hard to get to where I was, and I knew all my professors and colleagues would attest to that. How did my being a woman, an African or a black woman for that matter, affect anything? My ignorance suddenly turned to anger.

CHAPTER 20

I was almost thirty years old, married with two children and a master's degree from Cornell and a Ph.D. from Rutgers, before I knew I was black. For me, knowing I was "black" and having a dark skin color were two very different things. I was born on a Friday and named after my paternal grandmother so my birth name was Efua Seguah. My mom and my family affectionately always called me Naana. I do not know where the tradition started but I know that at the time I was born you had to have an English name to start school. Ghana, of course, had been a British Colony. My English name and therefore the names I would forever use in school and on all official documents was Emelia Ethel Ackah.

Ghana does not have many white people, but when I was growing up it was customary for Lebanese and Syrian businessmen to own shops all around the country. Yes, their color was different from ours, and they came from faraway lands. Having lived with them for years there was no longer the childhood inquisitiveness of running after white people, calling them "*obroni*" (meaning "white person") whenever we saw one in Kumasi. All the nuns at OLA Boarding in Elmina where I attended primary school were white. The novelty of "*obroni*" had worn off by the time I went to OLA, and I don't recall even taking any particular notice of their color at that point. If I did, by the time I went to Wesley Girls any illusion of the white person being different from us was long gone.

Most of my teachers for the seven years in secondary school at Wesley Girls High School for both my GCE Ordinary Level and Advanced Level programs were white from Europe or North America. There were a handful from Asia and other countries in Southern Africa such as Zimbabwe. A few other teachers were Ghanaians. My teachers were demanding, with high expectations for all students, and were caring and supportive across the board. We related to them with respect because they were older but did not hesitate to talk to them about anything that was brewing in our young minds. They were our leaders but most of them became our friends as well. The differences in color had meant nothing to me except sometimes we would make fun of the way they behaved or lived. We could not for the life of us understand why Mr. Spedding, our chemistry teacher, would be cooking when he had a wife. We would make fun of him among ourselves: What kind of man is he to cook himself? In Ghana wives cook for their husbands. That was the norm.

I had traveled to the United States, stayed with the Wielands and the other families, and had been at IITA with a lot of white expatriate scientists working collegially with all. I had been both at Cornell and Rutgers where it had not crossed my mind that there was a reason to do things differently because somebody was black or white. I had never thought that way.

Now this was hitting me with a bang. Why would anyone not want to recruit me because I was black when I had the requisite qualifications? Where I came from, there were Ghanaians in all types of high-level positions, and I would get a position I wanted in Ghana if it was not due to the political situation.

I had been completely naïve. I was not a student of history. When in secondary school we had to choose between history and geography, I went for geography. I had read about the slave trade. I grew up in Elmina where we used to spend a lot of time at the Elmina Castle. I had studied about the slave trade, which had transpired many decades before with Ghana as one of the key focal points for slave ship departures. I had grown up surrounded by all the old massive hilltop forts built mostly by the Portuguese as staging posts to hold slaves. Standing at the rooftop of Papa's Baffoa Lodge, I could look directly at both the Cape Coast Castle as well as another small fort within walking distance of Baffoa Lodge. Slave trade history and consequences of old were everywhere.

In both Elmina and Cape Coast, a large number of established families have fair skins, with European names such as Vanderpoye, Bruce, and Vandyke, whose ancestors we knew were white slave masters who lived and worked in Ghana and were involved in the slave trade. In the Ghana I grew up in, those topics were not openly discussed. You might overhear grown-up conversations but they were not stories that were widely shared and discussed.

I absolutely had no idea of what the ramifications had been of this slave trade on the lives of the Africans who had been taken to faraway countries and are now a sizeable population within the USA. This rude awakening was the start of a slow, long process of learning about the experiences of black people in America as well as the new concept that I was perceived not for who I was but by the color of my skin. I felt it was a very sad way to live.

With this new awareness I could recall and reflect on what my own interactions had been with black Americans since I came to the USA. I do not recall interacting with any black person during my stay in Jerseyville. No one in my sponsoring Jerseyville Rotary Club looked like me, and I definitely felt the keen interest and expressed enthusiasm by all the people I met in getting to know about me, my family, my history, and Ghana and Africa in general.

Ithaca, though, had been different. In all my lectures there were other students and friends who looked like me. Most, if not all, of my close friends were international students from all over the world. There were a handful of African Americans I knew and interacted with, but they were not my close friends or colleagues. The same was true at Rutgers where most of my colleagues and friends were white Americans from all over the country. We worked and studied together and hung out with each other at the student center and in each other's homes. Everyone I interacted with was to me an individual in their own right. Each one, though, was very different from me, and I did not place any particular thought to anything else apart from the fact that we were different people with different norms and experiences. On a personal level, I had no inhibition in reaching out to whoever I needed to interact with. The color of people around me to this point had meant nothing to me but a difference in how our skin color looked. I had no reason to give it any other thought until now.

My life was at a crossroads in America. If I was being perceived as a black person but not Emelia Timpo or Naana Seguah, then I needed to take a fresh look at the new place and find a way to adapt, however painful that might be. Clearly, I was being told by the community at large that where I ended up finding employment would be decided by the color of my skin and not by who I truly was. In that case with all white men interviewing me for these positions I was interested in, I was not going to get anywhere.

As I struggled to find positions in my field of study, my lab mates who, in my judgment, had not been as studious were suddenly finding several good positions. I had now been home for almost two years after graduation and my third child, Edem, was born at the same St. Peter's Hospital in New Brunswick. The pregnancy and birth with Edem were very peaceful and smooth. She was a great bundle of joy from the beginning, and Awoye and Emefa were delighted to have a little sister to play with.

Our lives were immersed in a large Ghanaian community in the New York/New Jersey area. We were hearing a wide range of stories from our friends about the racial stresses they had been exposed to and the changes they had had to make in their professional lives in the new context they found themselves outside Ghana. I heard about African doctors, engineers, and lawyers who were struggling to get positions and driving taxis in New York City. One of our new Ghanaian friends we had met when our children

Albert and the children in Somerset, NJ

were at the Rutgers Livingston Day Care Centre in Piscataway together had a master's degree in planning and was also struggling to find a position. We learned that if one had expertise in computer programming, the chances of getting a job would be easier.

I struggled personally on what to do. Why would I work so hard to obtain a Ph.D. if all I would end up being was a clerk typist? I started to have sleepless nights. I was always in tears and extremely irritable with everyone. I had no knowledge of typewriters, let alone computers. My back was against the wall, and it appeared I had no options. Despite my apprehension, I decided to take the evening computer courses being offered at the Somerset County Community College. For almost six months I took courses in basic computer science, and Cobol and Basic computer languages, as well as the data analysis courses SAS and SPSS.

I frequently checked the job bulletin board at the College where different vacancy positions were posted as received from employers in the area. Out of curiosity and with nothing else to do, I applied for a temporary secretarial position that was open at the AT&T office off Route 287 in Somerset. This was very close to our new home, and I figured I had absolutely nothing to lose. It did not take long to hear back from them for an interview, which was quickly followed up with an offer for a six-month temporary secretarial position to support one of the directors, Barbara Jaffe.

Now I was paying particular attention to peoples' colors and the significance of color on the possible roles and hierarchies within the job environment. Barbara was a wonderful white lady to work with. She marveled at my competence, confidence, and exceptional writing skills. I did not hesitate to tell her about my background and qualifications, along with my struggles in applying for jobs in the areas of my expertise. She assured me of her support in the event more permanent senior positions came up for which I could apply. The assignment was only for six months, and there were a lot of discussions about the breakup of AT&T. It meant nothing to me, and I was not going to get concerned about an organization I knew very little about and did not care to know. My frustration was boiling over but I kept my head down and did what I had to do.

The position at AT&T came to an end through internal reorganizations, and Barbara was moved outside the Somerset office to Bedminster or Bridgewater. I did not know these places; they could have moved her to any place and I would not have thought much about it. I only cared about no longer having a job. New Brunswick seemed to be bustling with activity during this period. New apartments and hotels were being constructed. One of our Ugandan friends from the Marvin apartments was working with the Urban League in New Brunswick. She called out of the blue to inquire if I was still looking for work. A new Hyatt hotel was about to be completed in downtown New Brunswick, and the Urban League had been asked to provide support in the recruitment of some of the workers. I jumped at it. We set up a process to recruit mostly low-paying jobs such as cleaners, housekeeping help, laundry room workers, and a handful of receptionists. The recruitment for senior level jobs was assigned to another established white employment agency in New Brunswick.

This three-month assignment provided some initial understanding of the American workforce and the salary structures in place. The salaries for the housekeeping staff we were recruiting were under three dollars an hour; that of the receptionists were not much higher. I was informed that the low salaries I was looking at for those positions were actually much higher since they would receive a lot in tips. In my mind tips were optional based on the perception of the service provided. No worker can project how much in tips would be made in the course of a week or a month of work; therefore I wondered why that was relevant to the salary to be paid to any worker. Most of the people we recruited for these positions were either black or Hispanic. The complexities of the American work environment were slowly becoming clear to me with each encounter about different workplaces.

While taking on these temporary assignments I was also looking out for better positions with my newly acquired computer programming skills. I had a daily walk to the Somerset library to scan through the newspapers in the Classified sections where positions were listed. I would make a periodic trip to Rutgers to check the various bulletin boards on the different campuses for any possible options I could pursue. I would come back home and send out as many applications as I could.

I was looking far and wide, even as far as New York City, and now understood the meaning of being overqualified and not having enough experience. For the computer analyst positions I was looking for, I removed all traces of my postgraduate education and only provided the information on my bachelor's degree, temporary assignments at Cornell, and the recent temporary positions in New Jersey. My spirit was slowly dying but I knew I had to persevere. I had three young girls to worry about. I had grown up seeing Maa working hard to support not only her children but other members of her family. I still didn't know what had transpired between Maa and Papa but I knew she did not depend on any man to feed her children. I had to strive not to be overdependent on anyone—even if it turns out to be a slow ride to get to where I needed to be.

On one cold and dreary day in the fall I received a telephone call for an interview in the New York City Department of Sanitation for a computer analyst position I had applied for months earlier and long forgotten. It was not particularly one I was looking forward to as it entailed a long daily commute to the city. I prepared and went for the interview anyway and was offered the position a couple of weeks later. This work entailed using SAS and SPSS to analyze the level of garbage collected in the different constituencies of the city and the volumes being deposited in the Fresh Kills Landfill, and how much was being incinerated. The landfill was immense, covering 2,200 acres in the New York City borough of Staten Island. You can smell the stench from afar and see hundreds of all types of birds flying over the landfill as you approach from other parts of the city. After three solid and long years after graduating with a Ph.D. in America, I finally had a full-time position, albeit not in the area I wanted and with no regard to all the years of hard work. This would not define me. As always, I took it in stride and organized my household and childcare, nursery schools, and afterschool pick up. Luckily, Sister Ama Benewa was still visiting with us from Ghana. She had come to help us with childcare after Edem was born and Maa was unable to come this third time.

The work was interesting, and the team of six analysts working together was young and vibrant. We were a mixture of white and black professionals, women and men who enjoyed working together. It took me back to the wonderful Cornell experiences of excellent collaboration and work environment where the color of one's skin was irrelevant, at least not in any way I noticed.

The color issue came in fits and starts. It was not a prevailing thought in my mind. It would come up if something particular happened, but I tried not to brood about something I had no control over. All the senior officials were men; a lot of them were of Italian descent and were a rambunctious crowd, full of laughter and comradery. Occasionally, some of the field guys would come to the office after showering and changing from their field work, and you would not recognize them in their regular clothes. It reinforced for me the importance of seeing people as individuals, not by the color of their skin, the work they do, or where they live. Humans are all people.

At times like this I would again wonder how there could be people who did not see me for who I truly was, but rather see me only by the color of my skin. I kept telling myself to do whatever it takes not to lose what I had grown up with, appreciating people for who they are and not by any skin color. It is their loss if they choose to see me that way. It took too much energy to think that way. I was building up a different set of skills, and I knew that could only be good for me down the road.

CHAPTER 21

New York City was novel for me in many ways. Our offices were downtown near City Hall, the Brooklyn Bridge, and Canal Street. My daily commute was on the New Jersey Transit from the Jersey Avenue station to Newark with a transfer to the Path train to the World Trade Center. I would then walk the twenty-five minutes to my office, stopping at the corner of Worth Street at the Roy Rogers to buy two of their delicious biscuits for my breakfast. Lunchtime would be on Canal Street for some Chinese food and to walk and shop at the numerous cheap goods shops all around. Canal Street had a range of shops selling 220-volt appliances for overseas destinations. Ghana was always at the back of my mind. I would stop in those shops periodically to check on prices for large and small appliances for the day when we would need to purchase them for our eventual move to Ghana after the political environment permits our return. Summertime lunchtime walks on the Brooklyn Bridge were always a delight as I marveled at the numbers of people all around and the incredible solid architecture of the city buildings all around us.

As much as I was enjoying working in the city, the stress of the commute and the need to be closer to home due to Albert's on-call schedules was also coming to a head. I started looking for work in New Jersey. It did not take long for me to obtain a position in the New Jersey Department of Higher Education as a program analyst within the Educational Opportunity Fund in Trenton. This position was very similar to what I was doing in New York except the data pertained to the performance of students and their retention and financial aid assistance within the forty-six colleges and universities in the state. I would be half an hour from home, readily able to take the children for their afterschool activities and enjoy time with the family instead of being on New Jersey Transit.

The Educational Opportunity Fund (EOF) Program, which had offices in all the colleges and universities in the state, provides extensive remedial academic support mostly to minority students, in addition to ensuring their financial aid and other supportive needs throughout their entire educational life in these institutions were met.

In a lot of cases the support provided was to augment what was not being received at home due to difficult family circumstances. In the majority of the academic areas the students were enrolled at colleges, they did not have the fundamental basic skills in English and mathematics and general education to be able to be successful in college. This revelation began a real eye-opening process to the broad disparities in the lives of minority students in the country. I could not understand how any student could graduate from high school without the requisite skills and how students could be moved from one grade to the next with the officials at all levels, knowing full well that they did not have the tools for success at the next level.

I could not constantly help but compare the learning environments these students were coming from to the education I had received at both *Mmofraturo* and Wesley Girls High School, especially at the latter. How can an environment in a developing country be so much more advanced in ensuring learning and development compared to the idolized country of the United States? This was truly baffling to me. The State Director of the EOF program was Dr. Kwaku Armah, also from Ghana. My immediate boss in the evaluation unit was Dr. Claudette Smith, originally from Jamaica. All but two of the fifteen-person staff in the EOF office were either black or Hispanic. However, within the larger Department of Higher Education, there were very few minorities, and those who were there were either part of the secretarial pool or in junior staff positions. Kwaku was the highest ranked black person in the department, heading a unit dealing with issues related to minority students.

The issues of race and discrimination were front and center in the work of EOF. It was a wonderful learning environment for me to begin to understand the underlying institutional racism that existed in the country, ensuring that minorities were consistently held back. I had experienced extreme racism in my search for work but what was becoming clearer each day was much broader and endemic than I had experienced. By this time I had become more enlightened on the issues of race and could now see the levels of discrimination in a lot of what was happening within the department, as well as in the challenges and discrimination being experienced by other EOF colleagues in the institutions they served within the state.

The issues of racism and discrimination were open topics of discussion within the EOF office on a constant basis. We would have minority students from some of the colleges as interns in our office and would provide guidance to them on course selection and tools to ensure success on a regular basis. Feedback from them on the guidance they were receiving from the guidance counselors in some of these institutions was appalling. Kwaku, in certain cases, would have to intervene and have meetings with the different college administration staff on these students. Rajade Berry became one of our constant interns during her entire four-year education at Rider College in nearby Lawrenceville. Being raised by her grandmother in Neptune, New Jersey, after the mother left the family and her children, she found a home in the EOF office. Although academically challenged when she started, with the support and extra academic support within the college's Basic Skills Program she was able to graduate, pursue further education, and obtain her Ph.D.

Awoye, Emefa, and Edem in Piscataway, NJ

The success stories of the EOF students were far-reaching. Some students would start their first summer in college so far back in basic reading, writing, and mathematics that they would spend a year or longer doing remediation to be on par with their contemporary white college level entry-level students. They would, however, excel and graduate with honors when they got a handle on learning and were buoyed by the support they were receiving through the programs. They would usually not graduate within four years but would stay in school much longer. They would, however, graduate and become indispensable members of the community as teachers, community workers, lawyers, doctors, and congressmen and women. Clearly, given the right opportunities and support, their innate skills came through just like they had for me when I was encouraged and surrounded with high expectations and all the necessary support to excel.

***

It did not take long for the Chancellor and other senior staff members to see my competence beyond the analysis I was doing within the EOF program. Before long I was promoted to be the Assistant Director for Grants Programs working under Nancy Style and later Penny Stone, both white women. They both could not rave enough about my competence and the level of my engagement and achievement in the Grants Office. After a year of working in a subgroup for the initiation and development of the Requests for Proposals (RFPs) on the new Challenge Grant program established by the Department to provide additional resources to colleges for new enriching programs focusing on undergraduate education, I was promoted again to be the Deputy Assistant Chancellor for Academic Affairs for the entire state of New Jersey.

I had learnt along the way that education was not necessarily the degrees you had attached to your name but how you use your skills and knowledge—no matter where you found yourself. After almost twelve years after receiving my Ph.D. degree, I had struggled through many work experiences and have been able to reinvent myself in an environment where I never would have dreamt I would be. It was a classic example of making lemonade with the lemons that have been thrown to you and savoring each step of the way, no matter how hard the road.

I was feeling professionally satisfied, finding myself in a place where I had supervision of other staff members with Ph.D.s, both black and white but mostly white. I had a wonderful white male supervisor, Dr. Frederick Kriesler, who believed in me and my skills, and we worked perfectly together. I knew throughout my evolution and ascent in the department that not everyone was happy for me but I truly did not worry about it and kept telling myself not to waste my energy on people who would constantly seek to bring me down because I was black. I would not allow them the space to occupy my mind, no matter how hard they tried.

Another dimension of race that became apparent to me in the New Jersey Department of Higher Education was the subtle rivalry between blacks who had immigrated from Africa or the Caribbean to the United States and those who had had ancestry in the United States from the slave trade. As Kwaku and I and other immigrant blacks were moving up the ladder in the department, there was a sense that we were being favored. We had not been privy to any such discussions on the part of the white hierarchy and thus could not substantiate any of those claims. However, as with other race issues, there is always an element of truth somewhere. Much later I learned that apparently, in general, people preferred to work with recent immigrants who are perceived to be more reliable and hardworking. For me there was no element of truth in that assertion. I had worked in the EOF office with a wide range of dedicated minorities from varied backgrounds, and each person had worked as hard as they could with the limited resources we had in the program. We all became lifelong friends. We were a real family.

CHAPTER 22

One can never truly forget one's lifelong ambitions. The dreams always creep up when you least expect them. By this time I had been blessed on a lot of fronts. I had a loving family with my sweet daughters all growing up and doing well. We had settled in our new home in West Windsor, New Jersey, which was very convenient for my work in Trenton as well as for Albert's position in the Rutgers Community Health Plan (RCHP) multidisciplinary medical practice group.

We purchased our newly built home at 4 Aldrich Way, West Windsor, and the excitement of having all the extra space and the girls in one of the top school districts in the state was palpable. I knew the importance of being in an enriching school district, which provided the learning environment we wanted for our children. Things were going well for us. We bought our burgundy Audi sedan, and we still had our old station wagon. The children settled in nicely at school. The entire Toll Brothers subdivision of Windsor Hunt with its elegant detached, four- and five-bedroom single family homes had only three black families. I noticed these details but did not let them dissuade me from doing what I thought was best for me and my family.

The West Windsor/Plainsboro school district was no different. The children, however, each had wonderful caring teachers. They were learning to play the piano, involved in softball and Girl Scouts after school, making new friends, and having fun. Within our neighborhood we had excellent neighbors. The Galbraiths had a daughter, Chrissy, who was our Edem's age; they would always be seen playing with other children in our backyard after school. Mr. and Mrs. Peretti were awesome neighbors as well. Mr. Peretti coached softball, and we would carpool with them for practice. Mrs. Peretti would pick up the girls, and they would stay in their house and play with their daughters Emily and Kathie till Albert and I got home. Emily and Kathie were contemporaries with Awoye and Emefa. It was a wonderful nurturing environment.

The first major blip during our West Windsor stay occurred almost a year after we had settled in our new home. We woke up late one Saturday morning, and I went out for my usual morning walk.

I crossed the lawn to the left of the house. On my return I stopped to open our mailbox and to settle in to read the newspapers for the morning. To my utter horror and surprise, the mailbox was covered with broken eggs. I was livid. Why would anyone do this to us? I walked up the driveway, and from a distance my eyes landed on the broken eggs sprayed on our Audi. As I got closer my heartbeat heavily increased. I was stunned at the sight of the letters "KKK" written in huge white letters on the trunk and on the front bumper of the car. I screamed so hard with fury and disgust, that Albert and the girls came running from the house. It was utterly disgusting. We all started crying from the sheer anguish of this intrusion in our sedate lives. Mrs. Galbraith was working in her backyard and came running over to find out what was happening. A few other neighbors who heard my screams came over. Albert called 911, and within minutes the police arrived to assess the scene and interview all of us gathered there.

The tumult of that intrusion on our lives never left me. I would always go back to my grandmother's perpetual reminder, *"Se obi se wu a, nya nkwa kyere no,"* meaning *"If someone wants you to die you need to live beyond their expectations for them to see."* There were a lot of friends and family members suggesting at the time that we move. They stressed that the area was going to be dangerous for us to live in, especially with young children. I was determined. We were not going to allow our lives to be dictated by hooligans who had no idea who we were and were acting out of their own limited and racist mindset. No, we would not allow that and should not allow that.

By this time I was definitely more aware of the extreme racism that existed in the country as a whole, and West Windsor was not immune to it. I had observed and heard other African American colleagues deliberate and ponder in meetings before participating. There was always an element of caution and analysis on how their actions and words might or might not be perceived. There was anguish in the perpetual analysis of the black versus white relationships. I was made to understand that was how it had always been for them. For me all this was new, and I was realizing as well the immense toll it takes on your mind and the energy spent on all the never-ending analysis of thought, word, and deed just for being black.

In my mind I determined I would do whatever I wanted to do and not spend my energy analyzing, especially about people who detest you to start with. I would be myself and continue to treat, love, work, and relate to all people the way I grew up, unless there was a reason to do otherwise. I was lucky to have grown into adulthood without this additional layer of mental strife and perpetual struggle. I had wonderful white neighbors and others who were very good friends. I had grown up and been taught by white teachers who cherished me, scolded me when necessary, motivated and inspired me for years. I was not going to fill my head with generalizations about the white race. But I was not going to be oblivious to the racism I saw all around me either.

In spite of the racial scare at our home, our seven-year stay there was to be one of the memorable times of our lives. Our home was the center of community activities for our Ghanaian friends where we hosted birthdays, weddings, and naming ceremonies, and had enjoyed the sheer fun of cooking and eating and talking in the company of friends and family. Friends such as Conrad and Eunice Bonsi would visit from Alabama and Vicky from Ghana among others.

CHAPTER 23

The statewide political elections of 1993 were brewing with ramifications for the Department of Higher Education. Christine Todd Whitman, the Republican, won the vote, replacing James Florio as the Governor of New Jersey in January 1994. Even before her inauguration the words and sentiments along State Street in Trenton were low-keyed and full of apprehension among state workers. They were not surprised when, within a couple of months of her assuming the helm of the State, major political decisions were implemented.

Whitman abolished the New Jersey Department of Higher Education, announcing she saw no value in having a state department overseeing policies for higher education institutions. A small core group was left to constitute a new Higher Education Commission for the state. The Higher Education Student Assistance Authority, which had the responsibility to manage both the federal and state student loan programs, was left practically untouched. Her administration did not see any value in having a statewide entity review academic programs, set guidelines for institutional accreditation, and provide any level of oversight to any institution.

The department operated differently with private institutions such as Princeton and Seton Hall Universities, most of which did not depend to any appreciable level on state level funding. For the community colleges and state colleges, however, most of their resources came from the state, and the greater engagement of the state on their overall programs and management had been lobbied against over a period of time by their leadership. Thus, the decision was generally well received initially by the colleges and universities. The staff were informed and provided with barely two months' notice, although there had been earlier rumors of this happening.

Another life-altering period was evolving right in front of my eyes. The girls were growing older. Awoye was in tenth grade at the private Stuart Country Day School in Princeton where she had started high school two years earlier. Emefa was in eighth grade at the West Windsor Plainsboro Middle School, and Edem had just started fourth grade at the Upper Elementary School. Albert was comfortably settled in at his practice at the RCHP.

By this time I was drained with the job searches in the USA. I had absolutely no more energy to scramble. Knowing the realities of the job market, I knew that if I were to start looking for other higher education positions, I would be told I did not have a degree in education or higher education administration so the frustrating job search saga would be repeated. I discussed with Albert the option of going back to Ghana with the children. They would go to school there, hopefully learning a bit more of the language and the culture after living there for much longer than the Ghana vacations we had taken years earlier.

I was dreaming about the potential of Wesley Girls High School for them. That would be a very different environment and a wonderful exposure that would stay with them for life. We thought about this option and decided it might be a good thing to do. We had to try it to see if it would work. Financially, it would be tough but Maa was home. When I discussed the option with her, she was elated and would definitely help us out as needed.

With the decision made I began an earnest search for work in Ghana with the public, parastatals, as well as the private institutions. I began to look at some of the international organizations working in Ghana as well. A number of years prior I had applied for different positions with the Food and Agriculture Organization (FAO) of the United Nations, which was more in line with my academic qualifications. I applied for temporary, short-term jobs, as well as permanent positions. I spoke with schoolmates who worked within the UN who confirmed it would be very difficult to get an opportunity without knowing someone in the system. Apparently, there was a lot of nepotism so potential competent candidates from developing countries were systematically not selected in favor of developed country candidates.

I listened to the guidance, sentiments, and stories from a broad range of people I felt were knowledgeable about the system. Most people would tell me about the almost impossible and difficult scenarios but were not willing to assist, mentor, and guide me along. I plodded along with my applications, for Ghana, the FAO, and other international organizations.

CHAPTER 24

In August 1994 I took my three daughters to Ghana. I had visions of them integrating into the same Wesley Girls High School environment that had been so endearing for me. Mom, of course, was beyond herself with joy for us to be close, although she lamented Albert not coming along. Albert was her darling.

We found comfortable housing in the Dzorwulu suburb near the airport. Views of the flights leaving Kotoka airport were always visible from our expansive veranda where we would settle each evening to relax, play *oware* or Ludo, or just do nothing. Surprisingly, settling down back in Ghana was not as difficult as I had envisioned. We had some savings in our pockets and, with accommodation sorted out, food was readily accessible. We had shipped our much-loved burgundy Toyota Previa SUV ahead of time. It cost over five thousand dollars to clear from the harbor but at least we were mobile.

Now came the challenge of finding schools for the young ones. The trip to Cape Coast to Wesley Girls was first. The then headmistress we met welcomed us warmly but explained that the Ghana school system had in the early 1990s been dramatically transformed into the Junior Secondary School (JSS) and the Senior Secondary School (SSS) system with each needing three years to complete. This was a complete revamp of the secondary school system I had known. Wesley Girls was therefore now a senior secondary school with admissions for fifteen- to eighteen-year-olds, and students were required to start from SS1 or JSS1. Awoye's correct grade level in the new system would be SS2 and Emefa's would be JSS2. Wesley Girls would not admit Awoye unless we were ready for her to repeat one year. This started our trek to other SSS schools, including St. Rose's, an all-girls boarding school in Akwatia, Aburi Girls on the Akwapim mountains outside Accra, Albert's alma mater of Achimota School in Accra, and SOS in Tema. In all these schools and others we visited the same story was being repeated. For Emefa we checked St. Rose's School in Akwatia and several others for the JSS options.

Finally, we found that Ghana International School (GIS) in Accra was the only school still pursuing the traditional secondary school curriculum. Being private and catering to the children mostly of expatriates, it had decided to continue with that model and enable students to sit for the Ordinary and Advanced Level Exams.

Hooray! To GIS we went. Mrs. Akilagpa Sawyer, the Headmistress, received us well. Both Awoye and Emefa would be eligible to attend GIS. She arranged for them to take the entrance examinations; both passed with excellent scores. Mrs. Sawyer explained that payment of fees would be in US dollars since the children were American, even though I had a Ghanaian passport. I agreed to pay in dollars.

The girls at the British School of Lomé in Togo

She kept telling me of instances in which Ghanaian parents like me coming from abroad had insisted they would pay in dollars only to start pleading with her after a semester to get the local fee rate. I assured her that would not be necessary in my case as I was sure to get a job soon, and my husband was a practicing physician in the States. I was in no way going to jeopardize my children's chances of getting the education we wanted for them. Over the following two weeks we kept calling, visiting, and waiting for Mrs. Sawyer's letters confirming the children's acceptance into GIS to start school by mid-September. She kept stalling, for whatever reason I could not understand.

Eventually, I gathered she could no longer take my persistence. She informed me that there was another similar school in Lomé, Togo, should I be interested in seeing if there would be possibilities there. Why was she sending us to Lomé, a two-hour drive, when the girls had passed their exams and she had initially confirmed there were open slots for their acceptance? I didn't know but we made the necessary appointments, I packed the girls, and off to Togo we went to the British School of Lomé (BSL) soon thereafter. This time we met with Mrs. Sayer, the British Headmistress who showed us the beautiful campus near the country's Presidential residence. We inspected the dormitories and the classrooms including their computer and science laboratories. The girls settled down to take their entry exams, which they readily passed again.

By the end of the visit their admissions were assured, a prospectus was given, and the date for them to return to start school was finalized. The school fees for BSL were more expensive than for GIS with deposits due on the first day of school. We were set.

Although BSL was not in Ghana and not Wesley Girls, the fundamental principles were all there. Both Awoye and Emefa loved the school and were happy to know that they could finally begin. Their school search had been anxiety-ridden from start to finish.

Even though I had written to a number of the schools in Ghana before arriving, it was as if I was literally starting the entire school search from scratch upon arrival. I went back to let Mrs. Sawyer know my girls had been admitted to BSL and they were happy to start in Lomé, Togo. She could not believe what she heard.

Only then did she say aloud what we had guessed all along. She was worried that perhaps I would not be able to afford the fees. The fees at GIS were one third that of BSL. We moved on to start preparations to get them to school.

I was left with finding a school for Edem who was only ten years old at the time. We did not want to start her so early in a boarding school. The load had been lightened but I geared up again in earnest. The possible schools near Dzorwulu were Lincoln Community School, Morning Star International, and Soul Clinic International. It was a much easier search with the lower grade levels. I decided on Jack and Jill School in the Ridge neighborhood. It was close to home so we would not be sitting in the morning traffic. The teacher for Edem's grade was an energetic young man who came across as hardworking, enthusiastic, and eager to impart knowledge to the young children under his care. With this decision made on schools, one of the key and critical tasks needed to settle us all down was done.

Maa took charge of getting the girls' prospectus lists ready. It reminded me of my preparation for boarding school many years ago. Maa loves to work hard, and for her grandchildren she was not going to leave any stone unturned. She sewed their bedsheets and matching pillowcases from the floral cotton prints she was able to get from the Makola markets. Provisions and toiletries filled the chop boxes she had her carpenter specially make in Kumasi and bring to Accra. Lovely summer dresses with frills were made, as well as the Ghana traditional outfits for Sunday church services and social occasions.

The day finally arrived. We now knew the drill at the border crossing. Maa already had her Ghana cedi notes ready to distribute for them to let us pass through quickly, which we did. We settled Awo and Emefa in their dormitory with Ms. Addy, their Ghanaian housemistress overseeing fifteen girls. By this trip we had found out that one of Albert's classmates and friend from Achimota, David Bampoe, was the Ghana Commercial Bank Manager in Lomé, and one of my *Mmofraturo* and Wesley Girls friends, Lawrencia Dzakuma, was also working in town. We allowed time to visit since both of them lived just a couple of blocks from the school in the affluent presidential quarter. They became the girls' local guardians during their stay at BSL.

The British School of Lomé served as a haven. As they tell it, Lomé was a close-knit group of classmates. There were around one hundred and fifty students in total, and everyone knew everyone else. As it was a small boarding school, they spent a lot of time with the same people in sports, at church, and in class, which led to lots of bonding and fun. The students came from all over Africa or, in fact, throughout the African diaspora as there were students from South America and other disparate places as well. It was a good environment with excellent teachers, which provided a rigorous education environment in which the girls thrived. They thoroughly enjoyed their time there, though it was a shame that afterwards the large band of students largely fell apart and went their separate ways.

CHAPTER 25

After settling Awoye and Emefa at BSL and with Edem in school as well, I began the hard task of finding something to occupy my time. One of our good friends from New Jersey, Narku Dowuona, had introduced me to his cousin Mr. Ebenezer Akwetey, who was at the time working with Amex International, one of the USA international nongovernmental organizations (NGOs), as part of my new job search. When I spoke to him in Washington, DC, before I left for Ghana, they were putting in a new bid for a project in West Africa from the United States Agency for International Development (USAID). I vowed to stay in touch with him should any possibility arise. He traveled often between Washington, DC, and Accra, and we agreed to get together in Accra on his next visit.

In Ghana, as in most places, knowing people at the right places is invariably the way to get anything done. I started looking out for my KNUST classmates who had established themselves in the Ghana system while I was away in the USA. I contacted a number of colleagues at the Agricultural Development Bank (ADB), the prime parastatal institution charged to lead the country's agricultural financing sector. At the time they were expanding throughout the country, and I hoped to get a position there. I contacted others at the different tertiary institutions, Legon, KNUST, and Cape Coast University about lecturing opportunities. As always, Maa directed me to a number of her Freemason associates to inquire on who they could connect me to.

In Ghana to find a decent job your college degree has to match very precisely the work at hand, even when you may have had practical work experience in a different field. Finding work as an analyst or in the ministry of education was a big stretch, although I had over ten years' experience in higher education management and policy development. My focus was to find a position within the agricultural sector. This was becoming an all-consuming effort. By the end of September 1994, I decided to stop the job search, relax, enjoy Ghana, and restart at the beginning of the new year.

As it turned out Fate was not going to allow me the respite. Out of the blue I received a call from Mr. Akwetey to inform me that Amex International had won the USAID bid. The project was designed to build the capacity of Ghanaian businesses to export nontraditional Ghanaian products. He wanted to check if I would be interested in working as a technical advisor based on my agriculture background as well as my knowledge of standards and quality assurance procedures that would be needed to help these farmers.

What a godsend. Of course, I was interested. I jumped at it, and after a couple of weeks of necessary paperwork I was in the Amex office setting up at the Ghana International Trade Fair Site. Before long the project team leader Peter Fraser arrived from the United States, and between the two of us we worked to recruit the additional staff including the national coordinator, the secretary, and the driver. Although it was a small office, it turned out to have tremendous outreach into the business community nationally.

Traditional Ghanaian exports were gold, bauxite, and timber. Some businesspeople, especially women, had started to grow pineapple, pawpaw, black pepper, and yams specifically targeted to the export markets, primarily in Europe. Interest was growing within the European Union to accept produce from West African countries. A number of entrepreneurs had procured large tracts of land for commercial production of pineapples and pawpaws, especially in the Nsawam area in the Greater Accra Region as well as in the Central Region. Others were heavily producing black and white pepper in the Western region beyond Takoradi where rainfall was consistent and necessary for these crops. A significant volume of these products being exported at the time were rejected on arrival in Europe due to poor quality control, undue delays in shipments, and inefficiencies in harbor operations leading to the decay and loss of large consignments of shipped products.

Our small team set to work in a hurry. Our office space had been provided by the Association of Ghana Industries (AGI), which also had their offices at the Trade Fair Site. Working in close collaboration with AGI, the Export Promotion Council of Ghana, the Ministries of Agriculture and Forestry, and the Ministry of Trade, we put together a two-year work plan to help address the pressing issues in the export of these nontraditional products. Building the capacity of the farmers and helping them set up necessary cooperatives to pool their efforts together to access both technical and financial resources became a main priority. Empretec, Ghana, became a key partner in the provision of the necessary training for the farmers and cooperatives as well as for all members of AGI.

In addition, Empretec was the leading institution for the training of micro, small, and medium sized enterprises in Ghana and had been established in 1990 as a public-private partnership project of the United Nations Development Programme, Barclays Bank of Ghana Ltd., and the Government of Ghana. At the time my good friend Felicity was the Deputy at Empretec under Alan Kyerematen. Since we knew both of them and their strong training competencies, we formed a solid group to implement all the training components of the project.

I enjoyed the work, especially the field trips to the farms and talking to their teams on the ground. We managed to get a German quality control firm to come and provide training to selected farmers on how to maintain the practices needed to be certified and designated as organic producers in the European markets. Understanding the importance of and benefits of collaboration instead of competition among themselves helped to pool their products together and reduce the processing and shipping costs among other things. The farmers were also able to collectively sell locally what was not shipped abroad in a way that ensured decent prices commensurate with their efforts. A number of NGOs working across the country were similarly engaged and trained, and we worked to establish close linkages. This was a different but very rewarding experience.

I was settling down nicely. Edem and I looked forward to our weekend trips to Lomé to visit with Awoye and Emefa. Eventually, some of our friends would join us for the trip to shop in Lomé where at the time prices for imported products were much less than they were in Ghana. Home is always home.

Before long December arrived. The girls were home, and Albert came for Christmas. After our separation in August, the Timpo Five were together again. We visited family and friends and entertained at home as well. The trip to see the family in Peki-Dzake was wonderful. One of Albert's medical school colleagues, Dr. Wuaku, was the physician in charge at the Akosombo Hospital so we stopped over and spent the day with him and his family. Together we went to the Volta Hotel and had lunch on the terrace overlooking the Akosombo Dam, the main power generator for the country at the time. We arrived in Peki just before sunset to meet the entire Timpo clan assembled in the family home to welcome us. Palm wine, the local brew tapped from fallen palm trees, had been pre-ordered for the customary libation to be poured, calling on the ancestors to drive away all evil spirits that would hinder or impair our stay and to ask the ancestors to bring good luck on all of us.

Albert's aunts, Tase Donkor and Tase Tomahase, were particularly elated to see our children who had grown so much since they last saw them. We spent the rest of the evening feasting on all the food delicacies—banku and okra soup with kelewele for dessert—that had been prepared and caught up on family news before retiring for the night. After two nights with the family, we returned to Accra for the Christmas festivities.

Time truly goes by quickly when you are having a lot of fun. Before long it was time for Albert to go back to New Jersey and Awoye and Emefa to go back to school. Little did we know that our lives were about to change again.

CHAPTER 26

One February afternoon in 1995 I received a call from the Food and Agricultural Organization (FAO) of the United Nations office in Rome. Its director, Mohammed Omar, informed me that he had seen my generic application for a position in the organization. They had a temporary six-month position for a partnership advisor position based at their headquarters in Rome, Italy, and wanted to inquire if I was interested.

It was so unexpected, and I didn't have a clue what that opportunity would entail for me and my family. I thanked him profusely and expressed my lifelong interest in working for the FAO but requested to have some time to discuss it with my family and return to him with my decision. Additionally, I asked for the details of the position and other application information to be sent to me for consideration. Mr. Omar informed me that they would send all the documentation through the director of the FAO Regional Office for West and Central Africa located in Accra and to liaise with him going forward. At the time I did not realize this was going to completely turn our lives around.

My heart was pounding fast, and sweat was forming on my forehead by the time I hung up the phone. I immediately called Albert with the sudden news and opportunity. I'm not sure how I blurted the news out to him. I could not think straight at that point. The excitement abated, and we put our thinking caps on after a day or so. I was currently in an excellent position that was scheduled for a period of three years and was being paid very close to what I was making at my last position in the New Jersey Department of Higher Education. Our children were all properly situated, and everything was going extremely well for them. Why would I leave all of that and take a six-month assignment that had no guarantee of continuing and disrupting all our lives once more?

It was a very tough decision to make. I consulted with some of my acquaintances in the United Nations in New York who knew how the system operated. I went to meet and talk at length with the director of the FAO Regional Office, who also confirmed what my friends were telling me. He, however, indicated that the position being offered was a brand-new consultancy position created by the new FAO Director-General (DG), Dr. Jacques Diouf, who had just started in his position in December 1994. Although there was no guarantee of a permanent position, there was a good chance the consultancy could be extended if my performance was deemed good.

Working with the FAO had been my dream job during all the years I was in New Jersey. I had submitted more than one hundred applications for different positions over the years with no feedback. I had even met with the head of the Ghana Mission to the United Nations in New York, Ambassador George Lamptey, to seek his guidance on how to get into the system, and he had spent a lot of time briefing me on the difficulties due to the national quota system. However, he had indicated he would seek further information and get back to me. I had subsequently called on him periodically to keep my request on his busy agenda. Now here I was with this opportunity and at a loss about what to do.

Albert and I tossed so many options in our minds. Eventually, we decided it was an opportunity not to be passed up despite the fact that there was no guarantee of a permanent position in FAO after the initial assignment. I knew I always worked hard, and I was committed to do the same wherever I was placed. This new position was to help develop new programs for the organization in four key areas: to broaden FAO's collaboration with academic and research institutions around the world, to initiate a Young Professionals program to enhance the participation of young graduates with master's degrees in FAO's areas of work, to enhance technical collaboration and share expertise between developing countries, and to enhance collaboration and sharing of expertise between countries in transition from the Soviet Union.

I prayed over this decision. With my profound experiences in both higher education and the FAO's focus on agriculture, forestry, fisheries, and land management, I felt I had the right profile to take on this assignment. After two weeks of intense deliberations, I called Mr. Omar to accept the offer. We agreed on a start date in May, indicating we would immediately start on the necessary paperwork, medical examinations, and initiation of service.

The Timpo planning started in full gear. Albert and I decided we would leave Awoye and Emefa at BSL since it was a boarding school, and they would come to Rome during their school holidays.

We would miss the weekend visits but we would find a way to make it work. Edem would stay in Accra to finish the school year while I went to Rome to assess the situation.

Edem's school was very close to the house of my good friend and roommate from KNUST, Felicity Acquah, who was working at Empretec. Both our moms were midwives in Kumasi and good friends as well. We decided to talk to Felicity and her husband, P.C. Acquah, to find out if Edem could stay with them till the end of the school year in July. Incidentally, P.C. was a good friend of my older brother Kodwo; they were classmates in Achimota Secondary School.

Felicity and her husband were elated to help. We'd been visiting each other during the time I was in Ghana, and their children and our girls knew each other and played well together. Edem was thrilled to stay with them. That would mean more playtime with both Kofi and Nana, their children. I was relieved. Next, we had to go to Lomé to relay the information to Awoye and Emefa and to discuss with them the new family travel and other plans going forward. Surprisingly, they received the information with a lot of curiosity and excitement about the possibility of visiting Rome. Since BSL was an international school with a lot of students from families working in different international organizations, they already knew of other children in their school who had parents working in different cities and countries around the world and traveling home for holidays. That was a relief. It suddenly was working out better than if they had been in a day school in Ghana.

Informing my work colleagues of my impending departure was difficult. We had built a strong and productive team, and we were being seen and acknowledged for all our contributions to the export industry in the short life of the project. The Amex team and AGI, USAID, and Empretec colleagues were all sad to see me leave. It felt almost like a betrayal to leave midstream, but this was an opportunity I could not pass up. I still had a couple of months before my May departure so we started a process to find my replacement as well as document all the aspects of the assignment that would be helpful for anyone who took over from me. We still had time to organize a series of critical training sessions prior to my departure.

Maa was disappointed since we had had more time together and done a lot together in Ghana. Although she lived in Kumasi, we had been able to plan for her to come to visit often, and I would go to Kumasi for a weekend whenever I had a lull in my work schedule and travel. I knew I was going to miss her in Rome. She was glad Edem would be around for her to dote on in my absence.

I had heard during one of my calls to Maa that Papa had had a stroke in Cape Coast and needed extensive care at the Cape Coast Hospital. I had planned to go and visit but was caught up with the ongoing FAO process. Soon after I made the decision to move to Rome, I traveled to Cape Coast to see Papa, who by then had been transferred home and was being cared for by nurses recruited by my older half-siblings who were overseeing his care. I would go back several more times to visit and spend time at his bedside for hours, even though he was unable to speak. His health continued to worsen, and on 19 March 1995 we received the news of his passing.

I was emotionally numb at Papa's passing. While I was filled with sorrow at his passing, at the same time I knew so little about him. He had been a very fleeting part of my life. I definitely was not close to him or felt his presence for much of my life. Yet I knew he was an important part of Ghanaian society and was acclaimed for his accomplishments, particularly in spite of his humble beginnings. To become the first Vice-Chancellor of Cape Coast University is not something achieved easily. I felt the loss of a great human being, however flawed he may have been as a father to me and my mother's children. I had felt the intense disparity of how his different children from different mothers were treated and wondered often why someone with his accomplishments and knowledge would do that. It was not for me to judge, not knowing what his reasons may be. I could only look at the few instances of our interactions and recall his encouragement and reminders about the importance of hard work and take that as enough.

For his funeral all his children gathered at Baffoa Lodge to say goodbye. The funeral service was held at the Varick Memorial AME Zion Church in Cape Coast, and Papa was buried at the Asokyeano cemetery near Cape Coast.

Out of Papa's death there would be other new beginnings. One of my half-brothers, Kwesi Osam-Pinanko Ackah—

affectionately called K.O.P. by all—whose name I had heard so much over the years came from Belfast, Ireland, for the funeral. I ended up calling him "big brother." He had studied medicine in Dublin, then married and stayed on in Belfast, Northern Ireland. The two of us bonded immediately. To anyone who sees us together you can readily tell we're siblings.

We spent a lot of time together in Cape Coast chatting about our lives and wondered why we had never met. We agreed we would stay in touch after Papa's funeral, which we have done. Out of Papa's demise I had found another loving and caring brother.

With the funeral over, I left for Accra to finalize my preparations and travel to Rome. I had envisaged moving to Ghana and staying there for a number of years with my children enrolled in schools in Ghana, all of us immersed in the Ghanaian culture.

However, for each step of my life I was realizing that what I have planned always ends up different than my expectations. After less than a year in Ghana I was suddenly moving to Rome to work with an organization I had always longed to work for. Now the chance had come but I was not mentally ready for the move. Besides, it was not a permanent position but a six-month assignment with no guarantee of permanence. After extensive discussions we decided it was worth the risk especially with the school situations settled for all the girls. Change never comes in a neat package, and I had to learn to deal with it with each opportunity. I was ready for FAO. I said my goodbyes to Awoye and Emefa at BSL the weekend before leaving for the new adventure in Italy.

CHAPTER 27

My position in Rome was as a partnership officer. This was a new title and position created by the newly elected director-general Dr. Jacques Diouf, who had previously been the Senegalese Permanent Representative to the United Nations. It was one of the key initiatives he was bringing to the organization, and its aim was to promote and broaden the collaboration between FAO and academic and research institutions across the world. He also wanted to set up a more systematic program to engage young professionals in the work of the organization.

For me, the position brought my academic expertise in agricultural science, especially tropical agriculture, and my professional experience in the higher education realm together in a way I would never have thought possible. It was a perfect fit, and I quickly got to work. It was a very small team under the leadership of Mr. Ramadhar, a true professional from India with impeccable writing skills. The other member of the team was Pedro Quetzal from Belize, with administrative support from Angela Swales from the United Kingdom and Louisa Sforza from Italy. Our unit was under the directorship of Mohamed Omar from Somalia who was a very close ally and confidante of the director-general. Omar had immense power and authority and was responsible for oversight of the management of all FAO's regional and country level offices.

It was a small group with a broad mandate that we had to deliver on quickly. We set to work and, despite the short time frame, began to show results. Mr. Ramadhar saw value in my request for meetings with the heads of all the key departments to understand their needs and priorities and assess how they wanted to best strengthen their ongoing engagement with academic and research institutions as well as to gain a better understanding of the possibilities and skills they needed in young professionals. This was one of the best lessons in my working life. I learned a lot in a relatively short time about the entire organization. I was known and recognized by the key leaders in the different departments, and my subsequent work was made much easier since I knew who to reach out to for whatever I needed.

Before long the team was able to develop detailed guidelines for the four main programs we were working on. Nothing works simply in a huge bureaucracy with a lot of layers of supervision and mostly men with extremely large egos. Everyone wanted to feel a part of the process and to let the DG and senior leadership know that they were also working on his priorities. Getting the buy-in from the departments was a challenge. It took some time but it was worth it. In the end the programs were very well accepted, and there was great enthusiasm to engage in the establishment of the needed expertise and experts' rosters and to use the information to enhance the work of the organization overall.

Yes, the work at FAO was an incredible opportunity. But that was nothing compared to the privilege of living in this ancient city for what would turn out to be a period of three years. I savored every opportunity. The FAO headquarters is located within a short walking distance of the Roman Colosseum, surrounded by so much history. From the eighth-floor cafeteria, one has a bird's-eye view of the Colosseum, the Roman Forum, the sparkling white national monument of Vittorio Emmanuel with the tomb of the Unknown Soldier, and the Palatine Hills. One can stay there forever marveling at the immensity of the landscape and the history that they evoke. From the back side of the same floor one can see the Roman baths of Caracalla with standing ruins of portions of the old city walls in full view.

During my first month in Rome I stayed at a bed and breakfast, The Lancelot Hotel, about a five-minute walk from the Colosseum. I could not have asked for a better location and a welcome home than this small family-run hotel with home-cooked dinners served to all residents as part of the stay. Everyone was warm, inquisitive, and friendly. Even though I knew not a single Italian word when I arrived, I soon became an expert in using sign language to navigate wherever I went.

My daily walks to work and back always involved stops at the Colosseum to take in the sights and to marvel at the ingenuity of those who lived there in times long past. I planned to learn as much as I could about the city and country since I had no idea how long I would stay. I walked through the streets of Rome whenever I had the time with no agenda and no idea where I was heading. I was enthralled.

With the help of colleagues from work and staff at The Lancelot Hotel, I found a nice one-bedroom apartment in the San Paolo section of Rome, three metro stops from the steps of FAO and within walking distance to the Basilica of Saint Paul Outside the Walls where the Apostle Paul is buried. The graceful cloister of the monastery of the church would serve as my Sunday respite location for reading. Such awe!

I felt blessed and privileged and had to pinch myself often that the experiences I was having were real. Such joy in my heart and so much ancient splendor everywhere I went. One of the most precious things I bought early in my Rome stay was a tour book that divided the city into eighteen sections, with self-guided tours one could take to cover each area in detail. This guide became my expert in navigating the history and marvels of Rome during my stay. I would dedicate several weekends to each section and return as needed to explore the magnificence of the architecture, churches, restaurants, and, above all, the lives of the people who lived in those areas now and in the past. I loved everything in and about Rome. I could not have enough of it.

During the week work progressed well. I had periods of anxiety about what would happen if I was not made permanent. However, after getting to know the organization, I was confident that even if that particular position was not permanent, I would very likely find another position either within FAO or the other agriculture related United Nations organizations in Rome such as the World Food Program and the International Fund for Agricultural Development. I felt my situation would stabilize; it was just a matter of time. I was patient but would periodically check in with Mr. Ramadhar if there was any possibility of getting the position extended or made permanent. My contract was extended a couple of times, and the process moved along. After a series of interviews, my position was indeed made permanent. My hard work had paid off.

Yes, I was working hard and enjoying the new city but I sorely missed my husband and my young daughters. I had this longing ache in my heart all the time. Deep down I felt something had to change for the family to regroup again in a way that kept us together. We would write letters all the time. When we had the chance, I would call and talk to each of them as much as I could, but it was not easy. We tried to keep our spirits up and pray that we would find a way forward. Once I had an apartment, we started planning to spend Christmas 1995 together in Rome. Our excitement was palpable. I began learning about travel planning and, with help from the FAO travel office, appropriate travel plans were made for us to congregate as a family again after almost seven months.

December came and we were all overjoyed to be together once again. We explored the city as much as we could and tried so many different Italian dishes. Across the street from my apartment was an amazing Italian bakery, La Fiorarini. We lived there, constantly going in for bread, pastries, and whatever else they might have that day. Between the bakery shop and the nearby ice cream shop, the girls always had delicious options to choose from.

Life in Italy is extraordinary. We had our local shops but each day there would be a fresh fruit and vegetable market in one area of San Paolo. Well-dressed women in dresses and pumps would slowly stroll by with their shopping carts, stopping at every stall to chat with the neighbors. No rush at all about

Emelia with friends in Rome

anything. I initially wondered why they would be all dressed up to go across the street to buy vegetables. But over time I began to appreciate the importance of true living and taking great care of oneself without the constant rushing and running I had gotten so used to in the United States.

Having secured a permanent position after over a year of temporary assignments, I was ready to find a permanent apartment in Rome. We decided to move out of the city center to the countryside and found a unit in a family-owned townhouse complex in Fioranello on the way to Castel Gondolfo, the Pope's summer residence. Fate was on my side. I found a perfect Italian family to live with. Two brothers had built the six-unit complex and shared it. The unit I rented belonged to the daughter of one of the brothers. Their papa lived in his unit next to mine, and he became the father I never had. He lived alone as the daughter, Alexandra, lived with her husband and young son in the city and would only visit on weekends. Papa and his family's Italian hospitality was beyond belief. We lived as was common to me in Ghana. Neighbors looked out for each other and counted on each other for support. Papa was in his late seventies and spent most of his time in the family orchard on the same compound, making homemade port and wine and enjoying the serene environment around him. He would ensure I had a plentiful supply of his port and wine whenever he made it and buckets of figs or tomatoes or whatever vegetable he happened to harvest at any time. His generosity reinforced for me the importance of learning about the people around you and believing that the more we looked out for each other, the better our own lives would be. Cultures are different sometimes but in a lot of ways they are closer to each other than we think.

During my stay Maa and I would talk regularly on the phone, and I was able to go to Ghana to visit with her a number of times. It was always a delight to be home, pampered and spending time with Maa in the afternoons sitting upstairs and playing *Oware* or *Ludo*, while she enjoyed her favorite Muscatella soft drink. I always wondered why she enjoyed it so much since she would always dilute it with water and complained it was too sweet. On one of my visits my younger brother, Nana Omiano, who stayed in the house with Maa, informed me that Maa was getting a bit forgetful. He was particularly concerned when a lot of times she would forget to turn off the stove after using it. We talked about it for a while, and I felt perhaps she was a bit tired and could use some rest. We decided it would be a good idea for her to come and spend some time in Rome, visit, and relax a bit. She was excited about it and could not wait.

I returned to Rome and immediately started making plans for Maa to visit. The FAO office provided all the necessary documentation to enable her to get a visa, and before long Maa was eagerly on her flight to Rome. She could not believe she was actually in the Eternal City with the Vatican, the Pope, and the Rome she had studied in history classes many decades before. She was beyond herself. I took some time off to show her some of the sights and, of course, Maa and my neighbor Papa became conversation buddies even though she spoke no Italian and Papa spoke very little English. A couple of months after Maa arrived Edem came to Rome on holidays so they kept each other company. By this time Maa knew her way around the shopping area in Sao Paolo where I used to live, and we would go there most weekends to do our shopping. I noticed, though, that she was beginning to get a bit irritable and forgetful. She had received her physical examination when she arrived in Rome, and the doctors had said there was nothing unusual for her age to worry about medically.

I thought perhaps she needed a bit of space and free time by herself, considering her usual independent streak. Thus, when she one day was eager to go out to Sao Paolo to spend the morning and asked to be dropped there on my way to work, I thought nothing of it and felt it was actually a great suggestion. In Italy all the shops closed at 1 p.m. and reopened at 4 p.m. in the afternoon. Thus, we agreed that I would drop her off on my way to work, then pick her up during my lunch hour and drop her back home.

At the main department store, Standa, there was a small garden with benches right across the street. We agreed I would pick her up at 1 p.m. If she was tired she could always wait on the garden chairs for me. Little did I know what I was getting myself into. That fateful morning she had her breakfast as usual and packed her fruits and other snacks. Then we drove off into the city. I dropped her off at Sao Paulo, waved goodbye, and drove off to work. When I returned at 12:50 p.m. Maa was nowhere to be found. I went into Standa and looked around but she was not there. I knew Maa loved to shop so I was not concerned. I also knew all the shops would soon be closing and she would come to the agreed spot. So I lingered around the area and waited for the shops to start closing.

One after the other the shops closed. By 1:15 p.m. they had all closed, and Maa was nowhere to be seen. The worry started. I got in my car and drove around the entire shopping area, down street by street, hoping to find her at a different spot from where we had agreed. Only a handful of people were out, the bustling had quieted down, and there was a still and eerie feeling in the air.

The panic set in. I parked my car again and started walking around asking anyone I met if they had seen a black woman dressed in a traditional African multicolored—green, brown, and red—long skirt and a matching top with headgear and carrying a small black bag. No one had seen her. One person thought they saw a woman with that description getting on a bus at a nearby bus stop. I ran in that direction and again asked the two gentlemen waiting for the next bus. She had not been seen. What was I to do? I was frantically looking everywhere and completely lost as to what to do. I walked back again to the front of the Standa, still with no luck. I had lived in the area and knew there was a small police station at the corner just by the Sao Paulo train station so I decided to go in there and ask for help. One of the policemen came out with me and walked around the area for a while, asking others we met if they had seen anyone with Maa's description. Again, no luck. The policeman suggested I check at home in case she had taken the bus home. I called Edem and her grandma had not been back. By 3 p.m. danger bells were ringing in my ears. I called my Ghanaian friend and FAO colleague Joana Maison Aidoo, who spoke perfect Italian, to inform the FAO security office.

I do not recall accurately how the rest of that day went. I remember hopping from one bus to another and one train to another. When I asked and someone said they saw someone like Maa on Bus/Train A or Z, I jumped on that bus or train to the end of the line asking everyone I met in case they had seen Maa. Joanna and other friends and colleagues joined in the search all over Rome. I was beginning to lose my mind.

Friends called Albert and my brothers in Ghana and London to inform them of Maa's disappearance. By the next morning, with the support of both the Italian Police and the FAO Security, Maa's photos were all over the city at the bus and train stations. There were radio announcements all over town about her. I did not recall eating or sleeping. I was roaming the Roman streets looking for my mother. What would people say if they heard in Ghana that Maa was lost in Rome? They would think I did not take good care of her. I was miserable to the core. We had to find her. I could not sit still and cried day and night. By the third morning I was beside myself. We headed back out to roam the streets.

As Edem and I and some friends started our now usual routine, Joana received a call from the FAO security that the police had informed them of someone who had just been brought to the Agostino Gemelli University Policlinic Hospital, one of the largest hospitals in Italy, and I needed to get there to cross-check if it was my mom.

I do not know how we got there. We arrived at the hospital and rushed through to the ward to find my mom sitting on a bed, cleaned up and smiling at me. I jumped. The first thing she said to me, with that beautiful smile of hers, was *"Naana na ekor henfa,"* meaning "Naana, where have you been?"

I should be asking that question! I just hugged her with tears of absolute joy. Everyone around was in tears. She had no clue that she had been lost for three full days in the city of Rome with a population of close to four million!

A short time later a doctor came in and explained to us that Maa had been found at the main Rome bus station, Termini, completely confused and incoherent. She diagnosed her with dementia. What is dementia, and what does it do to the mind? I had never heard of this disease or knew of anyone who had it. I just knew she had been forgetful but now I was being told she had a very serious disease that could progress rapidly over time. I was overwhelmed with fear and anxiety. My heart was racing. Albert had just arrived that morning from New Jersey, and it would take his calming presence and understanding of these medical issues to calm me down enough to hear what was ahead of us. Life's twists and turns were taking now an ominous turn I wasn't equipped to deal with.

CHAPTER 28

After Maa went missing in Rome, life was not the same again for her. I needed help with her care so we quickly arranged for Cynthia, who had stayed with me during my National Service at Winneba, to come to Rome to help with Maa. I could no longer leave her alone when I went to work or anywhere else. We were appreciating the gravity of the overall situation and the disease.

The doctors at the Policlinic continued to manage her situation and review her medication periodically. She could at times sit chatting and be like her usual former self, fun-loving and warm. Other times she would get very irritable and plead to go out on her own. We had learnt our lesson so that was not going to happen again. We could look back at some of her behaviors and realize that it was part of the disease, but I definitely did not have a clue about it.

All my time outside of work was now devoted to hanging out with my mom to make sure she was okay. We would go out for walks when the weather allowed and she was calm. Singing the Methodist hymns always brought her old self back so we sung a lot, and Papa would tell us how much he loved to hear my mom sing. She used to be a choir member at the Methodist Church in Kumasi and had always enjoyed singing. We found a piece of her past life that brought her immense joy.

One late August afternoon we took Maa to the Laurentina area for a walk. She was filled with joy. She wanted a particular green grape she loved, which we picked up for her from the farmers market in the area. We were not out for long. When we got back home, she complained of being a bit tired so went straight to rest after lunch. We suddenly heard her screaming. After running to her room, I found her complaining of a very bad headache. We called the ambulance. At the Salvatore Mundi International Hospital she was examined, and the doctors confirmed that she had had a bad stroke. She was kept in the hospital for about six weeks.

Again, Albert and other family members came to Rome to visit and help out. The outpouring of love and support from family and friends near and far was truly overwhelming. I was now hearing of other families' experiences with dementia and stroke and the ravages of high blood pressure and other diseases. I was learning about growing old. The doctors recommended that she be in her own usual environment surrounded by more friends and family instead of in Rome. I did not want her to go back to Ghana but eventually I was convinced that was for the best. In July 1997 I flew back to Ghana with Maa and settled her at home under the care of different doctors.

We organized a twenty-four-hour nursing shift for her. Sister Ama Benewa was also there to cook and provide any other needed support. The nurses were incredible, playing her favorite *Oware* and Ludo when her mind and body allowed. She was as comfortable as she could be. It was difficult for me to leave her. I was emotionally drained and at a loss as to what else was coming down the road. With much sorrow and apprehension and a tightness in my chest I had never felt before, I left Maa in Ghana and headed back to work in Rome. I would periodically go back home to see her and spend time with her, although she was beginning to slowly forget who I was. Life can be very difficult.

My life in Italy was reminiscent of life back in Ghana where communities took responsibility for each other and cared for the needs of its members regardless of whether they were family or not. The tennis court in Fioranello was one of my favorite stops on weekends. When the children were around, we would always be there playing each other and having a blast on the numerous clay courts. The owner of the club adored us, and we would always chat before we left. He called Emefa "a gazelle" and raved about her graceful tennis shots and easy manner on the tennis courts. He would often tease me about my weight and encourage me to lose some if I wanted to get better at my game. I marveled at the fact that people unknown to me would dare to comment about my weight. But for him it was nothing, and I knew and felt there was no harm intended but a genuine interest in my welfare and my joy at playing tennis.

By the time we were leaving Rome we knew and felt that "Africa begins in Rome and goes south."

With a lot of perseverance, hard work, and a willingness to adapt to the changes around me, I had many additional and exceptional opportunities beyond my assignment in Rome. I was appointed the Country Representative for FAO to Namibia. I had learned along the way the importance of opening my mind and my eyes to learn from those around me. I had a number of senior Africans in FAO who had mentored me during my tenure in Rome, and I appreciated their guidance as I worked within the intense bureaucracy of this huge organization. These included stalwarts such as Dr. John Monyo, director of the Agricultural Support Systems Division, and Dr. Keya who was the representative of the Consultative Group for International Agricultural Research (CGIAR) institutions to the FAO.

I joined a large African social group and worked closely with my dear friends, Juliet Aphane from Swaziland and Mahazosoa Ratsimba-RaJohn from Madagascar, to organize Friday and weekend social events for the group. My very close friend Martha Kassa from Ethiopia and I would wander out of Rome periodically, sometimes as far as Istanbul, for short trips to explore Europe. In fact, in the absence of my family, I created a new community and family that provided support and care.

Upon my appointment I walked into Dr S.O. Keya's office and asked for his guidance. We spoke about a lot of things. He had been the Vice Chancellor at one of the universities in Kenya and had held a range of other leadership positions. There was a lot I had already learned from him and knew there was more to learn quickly before leaving for Windhoek. One of his pieces of advice that has stuck with me since is that in a leadership position overseeing a broad range of people, I would often be pressed to sign a wide range of documents. He cautioned that my signature anywhere reflected my agreement to whatever I signed. I should never feel pressured to sign anything before I have had a chance to read it myself. I had to make the time and sometimes delay signing in spite of being told it was urgent and an emergency until I had read it. That advice served me well everywhere I went after Rome.

I was learning to say goodbye to wonderful relations and friends at this stage of my life. I was always emotional, but I also made up my mind that no matter where I went it was important to stay in touch with the key people with whom I had been close. I had not realized at the time how much energy and effort that would demand of me but in the long run that decision has served me well throughout my life.

In 1998 when I arrived in Namibia, HIV and AIDS were

raging with no anti-retroviral drugs. There was so much desolation. One would walk on the main street in Windhoek, Independence Avenue, where my office was located, and be able to visibly identify those who were suffering from AIDS.

As the FAO representative in the country, with oversight of all FAO offices and activities in Namibia, I had the responsibility to lead the efforts to improve the availability of FAO technical assistance to the Namibian Government and to assist in the achievement of their national development goals. My office coordinated the collection and dissemination of information to guide government-led programs, promoted national and international action to improve agricultural production and standards of living, and assisted in the provision of technical assistance to the Government of Namibia.

My focus ministries included the Ministry of Agriculture and Water Resources, the Ministry of Fisheries and Marine Resources, the Ministry of Forestry, and the Ministry of Land and Natural Resources. With the limited team in the office and technical support from both the headquarters in Rome and the sub-regional office in Harare, Zimbabwe, I was able to oversee the provision of day-to-day technical support to the ministries on issues including date production, reforestation, education programs, and fisheries in spite of the ravages of the AIDS epidemic.

Within the United Nations Country Team, however, we could not take our eyes off the impact of HIV within the society, and each office looked for opportunities to help the government on different scenarios to ensure prevention messages were reaching the entire country, especially in the impoverished communities in the northern Oshikoto, Okavango, and Kunene regions where the large black population lived.

Most families owned livestock, and over time most farmers were losing their cattle in large numbers by selling them off for funerals. Children were dropping out of school due to the sudden death of both parents and with no other relation to continue to support them. The fisheries sector along the coast in Walvis Bay was becoming decimated due to the sudden illness and deaths of a large number of their staff who mostly moved to the coast to work from the north.

The Dean of the Agriculture Faculty in the University of Namibia and the National Project Coordinator of an FAO technical support project, Professor O. Mwandemele, and I put our heads together and carried out a series of studies on the impact of HIV/AIDS on the agricultural and fisheries sectors in the country.

At this time HIV and AIDS was primarily considered a health

Emelia greeting Namibian President Samuel Nujoma
at a function in Windhoek

issue on the global agenda. However, on the ground we could see the immense human, social, and economic dimension of the epidemic across all sectors in Namibia. On one Saturday evening I was called urgently to the Windhoek General Hospital where one of my administrative officers had suddenly been taken seriously ill. The doctors and nurses on duty were unwilling to take care of her. I went in to talk to them and to find out how she was doing. I had seen her in the office the week before and had not noticed anything wrong with her. As it turned out they had tested her, found her to be HIV positive, and were pushing her to leave the hospital and go home since there was nothing they could do for her.

I was furious and gave them a piece of my mind. What was the point in them working as caregivers in the hospital if they were unwilling to take care of the sick? After much discussion they realized I was not leaving until they had admitted her and provided her with the necessary medication they had to make her comfortable for the night. Our chief driver in FAO, Emmanuel, lost his twenty-three-year-old daughter to AIDS. The Saturday when we attended her funeral we saw seventeen coffins lined up in the front of the church, of which only two deaths were due to non-AIDS causes. We knew something had to be done urgently. It was so depressing.

Emelia and President Samuel Nujoma at an event on date palm production in Namibia

Soon after this funeral the Executive Director of UNAIDS, Dr. Peter Piot, visited Namibia to personally assess the HIV situation and provide guidance to the president and other leaders on known modalities for prevention, care, and dealing with the rampant stigma and discrimination. He was so impressed with the data we had been able to collect and the reports we had prepared and shared within the country and within UNAIDS. The FAO team, in addition to the entire United Nations Country Team, was able to further discuss our observations at length with him on the ravages to the society at large we were seeing in Namibia. He had seen and heard similar stories across the world, but Namibia, with a population of just over a million people and having recently attained independence in 1990, was a special case of interest.

CHAPTER 29

On the morning of 3 July 1998 I received the phone call I knew would come but had been dreading. Maa's health had been declining over the past month; the doctors had indicated we needed to continue to make sure she was comfortable but there was not much else to do for her. I had gone back to Ghana to see her a couple of weeks before and saw she was not doing well. Now the inevitable had happened. I could not cry enough. I was beside myself with grief. My anchor and never-failing Maa was gone. One constant shining angel in my life was now dimmed forever. I flew quickly to Kumasi on a short trip to organize the customary one-week

Emelia and her brothers at Maa's funeral

celebration.

A funeral is an occasion to bring people together from both within and outside the family. They come together to mourn and say farewell to their dead friend or relative. The one-week celebration takes place usually the week after the death. This custom apparently came about because in the old days for at least one week the family would store and prepare the body for burial. With the modern advent of refrigeration, bodies are often stored for much longer.

During the one-week anniversary of the death, the extended family plans the funeral and lets everyone know the detailed plans that the family would be working on. Other decisions revolve around the food, drinks, and water for mourners and loved ones, sound

Emelia and her extended family at a Thanksgiving service after a funeral

systems, casket, plot of land for the grave, and several other items.

Maa's funeral was held at the end of August with a celebration of her life and achievements. In addition to family and friends that had gathered from all across the country and overseas, there were representatives from the Social Welfare Department, Kumasi Municipal Authority, and numerous other organizations she had volunteered with over the years. Parents and children she had delivered in her maternity home came from far and wide to celebrate her generous spirit and caring manner. On Saturday 29 August 1998 she was buried at the Tafo cemetery, two months after her death. She had touched so many lives. For me, a day would not go by without thinking of her. She would forever be cherished in my heart.

Emelia and her brothers

CHAPTER 30

Not long after Maa's passing and after Peter's return to the UNAIDS headquarters in Geneva, I was surprised to suddenly receive a call that I was being considered as the country representative of UNAIDS to Ethiopia and the liaison officer with the African Union and the Economic Commission for Africa based in Addis Ababa. Albert and I moved not long after this for me to start my new position. Ethiopia was a very different experience from Namibia. It was a much bigger country with a population of more than sixty-seven million people. Its capital, Addis Ababa, had long hosted the headquarters for the African Union, (AU), the continental-wide organization for all fifty-five countries. The African Union, much like the European Union and other regional bodies, was the key institution working to promote peace, security, and stability on the continent as well as promoting the acceleration of the political and social-economic integration of the continent.

Emelia speaking at UN conference

Thus, a lot of my work involved engaging in the interagency collaborative work with the other regional organizations based in the country. The AIDS epidemic here was no less rampant. There was pressure also on the AU at the time to strengthen its engagement on the raging AIDS epidemic on the continent. With the support of Secretary-General Kofi Annan and a number of other global leaders, the AU spearheaded the development of the Abuja Declaration on HIV/AIDS, Tuberculosis and Other Related Infectious Diseases in 2001. When African Union member states met in Abuja, Nigeria, in April 2001, they committed to allocating fifteen percent of their government budgets to health. This action was tremendous because more resources were required to address the pressing health challenges of the day; it demonstrated the commitment of the African leaders to do their fair share in this major effort. I was the UNAIDS focal point for the discussions and negotiations that led to this declaration and worked in close collaboration with donors, national government representatives, civil society organizations, and other UNAIDS colleagues and leadership to negotiate the development of the Abuja Declaration.

In addition to these continental wide efforts, the need to engage different Ethiopian communities in their national HIV advocacy and prevention work became a key priority for my office and the team. The need to empower women in the different communities to assert their right on sexual issues with their partners took on a different meaning due to the lower status of women in the social hierarchy. Knowing that most women spend a lot of time together each day preparing and sharing coffee within their social networks, we focused a lot of HIV prevention meetings for them around these "coffee ceremonies."

Working in close collaboration with the head of the National AIDS Council Secretariat, Dr. Dagnachew Haile Marian, and his team, we worked to strengthen the coordination of the national program across all the regions in the country. We created more effective mechanisms for their work with the civil society organizations and brought into the national dialogue more streamlined representation of the private sector, youth groups, women's organizations, and other donors that had previously been working independently. These efforts to enhance national program coordination would later bear tremendous results with the initiation of the Global Funds for AIDS, Tuberculosis and Malaria program launched by the global community to provide considerable funding for AIDS to developing countries. I was also able to secure funding for the UNAIDS Ethiopia office from a number of the international donors in-country to strengthen women's civil society organizations on their work with AIDS.

My work in Ethiopia also involved the collaboration with other United Nations organizations in the country, especially the International Organization of Migration and the World Food Program, to carry out a major assessment of the impact of HIV and AIDS within the internally displaced populations. With the 1998-2000 conflict between Ethiopia and Eritrea as well as food security challenges due to drought, the country was dealing with numerous humanitarian issues. The entire United Nations system, under the resident coordinator, was engaged in providing coordinated support to these communities.

I found Ethiopia to be such a beautiful and varied country. I made time to leave Addis Ababa and explore other parts of the country. During the holiday breaks the children visited, and we would travel to the northern part of the country to explore Azum,

Emelia with Michel Sidibe, UNAIDS Executive-Director

Lalibela, and Mekelle. Lalibela in the Amhara region of northern Ethiopia is a UNESCO World Heritage site, known for its distinctive rock-cut churches dating from the twelfth and thirteenth centuries, which are pilgrimage sites for Coptic Christians and considered to be the eighth wonder of the world because they have been carved completely out of a single piece of volcanic rock. The eleven churches in the area were built over twenty-three years during the rule of King Lalibela. The popular churches are Bete Medhane Alem and the cross-shaped Bete Giyorgis (Church of Saint George). Many of these churches are joined by tunnels and trenches, and we were awestruck to see such magnificent history enfolding in front of us. We also spent time around Lake Tana (the main reservoir for the Blue Nile) to the northwest and also in Bahir Dar in the south.

During my tenure in Ethiopia Michel Sidibe from Mali joined UNAIDS as country and regional support director. Until then Michel had been a senior executive in the United Nations Children's Fund (UNICEF). Up until that time posting staff of African descent as representatives for the different United Nations organizations to countries and regions outside of Africa was rarely done. Most Africans, when appointed as representatives, would be sent to other African countries. Michel advocated and helped change that dynamic in UNAIDS. Thus, it was an unusual and bold move by Michel to send me to South Asia, not as the head of one country office but rather as the head of the entire South Asia region, overseeing and coordinating the work of the countries in the entire sub-region.

***

After a three-year period Albert and I moved from Ethiopia for me to head the UNAIDS Intercountry-Team for South Asia based in New Delhi, India, and with leadership and oversight of the UNAIDS work and country office teams in Afghanistan, Bangladesh, Bhutan, India, Maldives, Nepal, Pakistan, and Sri Lanka.

The AIDS epidemic in South Asia was being fueled by men who have sex with mem (MSM) as well as injecting drug users (IDUs), although transmission through heterosexual unprotected sex was also of grave concern. The leadership in the region through the South Asian Association for Regional Cooperation (SAARC) was beginning to address the issue at the regional level. Most of the countries had effective national AIDS commissions with very good leadership through their respective national strategic plans prioritizing their interventions and allocating resources, albeit inadequate, to their programs. The UNAIDS support therefore focused on advocacy work to ensure the prioritization of the marginalized MSM and IDU groups that were fueling the epidemic. The advocacy sought to also address the specific needs of women, especially in the rural areas. With the large national populations in some of the countries in the region, we engaged with key parliamentarians, established civil society organizations, and the private sector, as needed, to raise awareness and to reduce the stigma associated with AIDS in general. We were lucky to have Dr. Nafis Sadik, who was then the Secretary-General's Special Representative for HIV and AIDS for the Asia Pacific region. Dr. Sadik, a Pakistani who had previously been the Executive Director for the United Nations Population Fund, (UNFPA), was well known to the heads of States in the region, was respected, and had dealt with issues of women and sexuality for years. She therefore became a key partner for UNAIDS work in the region. Through the collective effort of the United Nations Teams in the region and the respective national AIDS programs, key reports on the successes and challenges of the AIDS programs were documented and shared in the sub-region. In India, the first-ever India Parliamentary Forum on AIDS, spearheaded by Mr. Oscar Fernadez, a member of India's parliament, was organized, which was a truly historic meeting with more than one thousand and five hundred elected representatives in attendance.

My work involved a lot of travel to all the countries I was covering except Afghanistan. Each time travel plans were made for Afghanistan it would be cancelled by the United Nations teams in the country due to security reasons. I was, however, able to visit all the other countries repeatedly and appreciated the people and the different cultures in the region. Each country had its own unique character, and I felt blessed to have had the experience to visit, enjoy the wonderful cuisine, and share life experiences with a varied group of people from all walks of life. Meetings with the women groups in different communities were always of great interest to me. I was particularly amazed at the level of coordination and work ethics seen, for example, in the development of the local fabrics in Bangalore and Karnataka. Family groups were paid to develop specific fabric patterns in their homes using genuine natural dyes and hand stamping tools. These women cooperatives work together to meet the demands of larger companies in the local areas on a seemingly never-ending work schedule. As part of our HIV prevention work, we were able to identify selected groups to train on prevention issues, to encourage them to assert themselves in asking their partners to use condoms, and to become champions within their communities on HIV and AIDS advocacy for women.

Emelia in India

Awoye, Emefa, and Edem would visit a couple of times while we were stationed there during their holidays, and we made sure to see the key attractions of the country including trips to Agra for the Taj Mahal, Jaipur, and Mumbai. Exploring the expansive and sense-stimulating markets in

New Delhi and shopping for jewelry and clothes became a wonderful pastime. We were surprised to find shops in New Delhi that sold the traditional wax clothes that were used in Ghana at very reasonable costs. In reality, there was nothing that could not be found in the markets in New Delhi. All the shops were overflowing with goods, and in each shop you visited the owner would want you to sit down while they showed you their wares. You could easily spend hours in the markets without realizing it. The girls loved riding in the rickshaws, which were my regular mode of transportation outside of work.

India also brought back memories of my boss in FAO, Mr. Ramadhar, and to some of our conversations about their culture. In India, we learnt about the different caste systems and its impact on the lives of large groups of people. Different classes of people were designated to carry out only particular work. Thus, when the office driver dropped me off at home, he would not enter the house as a matter of routine even when I insisted he come in. He said it was the duty of the house help to collect anything we brought home from him at the door. In the three-story apartment complex where we lived each household had a helper in the house who only did work inside the house. Thus, we needed to recruit another person whose sole job was to sweep the stairs but not work inside any of the apartments. I found that very difficult to understand and would marvel at how the caste system had been so systematized in all walks of life.

One area I was completed impressed by was the organization and functioning of the Indian Administrative Service (IAS). The top achievers in each graduating class from college throughout the country, regardless of disciple, were pooled together and trained to be leaders as part of the country's administrative government. They would be assigned over a period of years to different line ministries in various regions of the country. Over time they would have an excellent knowledge of the entire country as well as a solid grasp of managing any national line ministry. These competent professionals become the backbone of the government managing the extremely complex country. South Asia was an incredible incubator of knowledge and beauty. There was so much to learn and appreciate in this region. The natural landscapes of the countries were beautiful and varied. From the idyllic sparsely populated Himalayan mountaintop country of Bhutan and the twenty-six atolls of Maldivian islands to the densely populated Bangladesh, Pakistan and India, all our senses were constantly being stimulated by the sounds, smells, and historic cultures of the people in the region. I marveled at the two thousand Hindu temples in Varanasi in Utter Pradash and the artistic ingenuity of the Khajuraho Monuments, a group of Hindu and Jain temples in Chhatarpur district, Madhya Pradesh, India, In the historic capital of the Himalayan country of Nepal, we lingered through its religious monuments, temples, monasteries, and stupas that stood out in the city's landscape, shopping for silk and linen in the process.

There was so much to see and appreciate in these countries but never enough time with the work that needed to be done. Before long we would move again in our migratory work pattern, this time to the UNAIDS headquarters in Geneva, Switzerland. I would become the associate director of country programming and liaison. I had come full circle and now had a similar position to what Mr. Omar had in FAO at the time I was first recruited to the United Nations.

Emelia, Albert, and the girls

With my team of twenty-five staff members, we supported the efforts to streamline our UNAIDS country and regional level presence through the establishment of seven new Regional Support Teams in Eastern and Southern Africa, Western and Central

Africa, the Middle East and North Africa, Eastern Europe and Central Asia, Latin America, the Caribbean, and the Asia Pacific region. I supervised all divisional staff and led regional coordination efforts pertaining to programming and planning, advocacy, strategic planning, budgetary, human resources, and other administrative matters.

One key achievement in my time in Geneva was to help coordinate the development of the "Three Ones" principles around the HIV and AIDS programs in countries. The principles are: one agreed AIDS action framework, one national AIDS coordinating authority, and one agreed country-level monitoring and evaluation system. Working with a team of colleagues throughout the organization and elsewhere, we developed these principles to enhance the effectiveness of the

The family in Egypt.

national AIDS programmes by streamlining the technical, financial, and human resources provided by all partners in all program countries. With the overlapping priorities and resources of different partners in countries, countries were getting overwhelmed with the number of partner-initiated meetings and requests that were then interfering with the implementation of the national program priorities. The "Three Ones" was launched at a meeting in London, hosted by the Department for International Development (DFID), and its use in countries served to foster better coordination over time.

***

Prior to my retirement my last posting was to the UNAIDS New York office as a senior advisor, and I led UNAIDS staff in the United Nations Development Group (UNDG) in developing guidance to streamline and promote reform and coherence in the entire United Nations system's overall support to country and regional level work. The UNDG ensured that the contributions of the UN system through the work of the UN Secretariat, the UN Funds and Programmes, and the specialized agencies were effectively streamlined to optimize the delivery of its mandate to its Member States. Most of the staff working at this level have had prior country and regional level experiences. Thus, recommendations for changes in both systemwide operational modalities and program management of the different United Nations system organizations were dealt with based on practical experiences from the field. Staff from different country and regional levels were also systematically brought into the dialogue to ensure their voices were being heard and that issues were being adequately addressed at the global level.

I was also the lead focal point for UNAIDS work in other areas such as integrating disability into our work and the social dimensions of climate change on our HIV populations among other areas. The work on disability was one of the most rewarding areas I had been involved in during my tenure in the United Nations. I was exposed to the day-to-day challenges faced by persons with disabilities in accessing both HIV prevention and AIDS care at a time when AIDS treatment options had become available. This work required urgent attention to quickly bring the adaptive changes needed to the forefront of the HIV and AIDS communities at large. We championed the inclusion of discussions in both plenary and small group sessions on the challenges faced by persons with disabilities and the possible opportunities that could be provided in all regional and global conferences. We had the support of a number of donor countries, and we worked closely with associations of persons with disabilities in North America and beyond.

The family visiting South Africa

CHAPTER 31

What a stretch. I had come so very far from the person with a Ph.D. working as a secretary at AT&T. None of it would have been possible without the unfailing support of my husband, Albert, and the flexibility and resilience of my dear daughters Awoye, Emefa, and Edem. With all the changes going on in my work life, moving across the globe with ever increasing responsibilities, the glue that held it all together was my family. The chaos and the instability of the repeated transfers were affecting all of us but we tried to make it work as best as we could. It was not always easy. The stress was palpable, and the sacrifices we each had to make to get through all those years left some dark marks.

Edem, after a year attending Jack and Jill in Ghana, moved to the British School of Lomé to join Awoye and Emefa for a year.

Edem at her Madeira High School graduation

Albert and I realized that transitions were going to be the norm in our lives, and we needed to make some longer-term decisions to keep the family together. The boarding school option was appealing as it provided stability in the day-to-day lives of the girls. Both Albert and I had attended boarding schools—Albert at Achimota School and I at Wesley Girls High School—and we both grew up feeling the immense benefits of that exposure. We decided to strive to help the children through that process as best as we could. The option of moving with them through the possible duty stations on an ad hoc basis was not tenable; in talking to other United Nations colleagues it appeared that boarding schools were the option most parents had adopted that seemed to work reasonably well.

    After two years at BSL Awoye moved on to Ohio Wesleyan University, and Emefa moved to the Phillips Exeter Academy in New Hampshire for two years before proceeding to my alma mater, Cornell University. Edem had a more tortuous route. After her sisters left BSL and with me moving to Namibia, we felt it best for her to join me and attend the prestigious Windhoek International School. She loved it and blossomed during her two years there. For high school, however, we decided it was best for her to have a stable high school experience. We were lucky to get her admission at the Madeira School in Mclean, Virginia. Madeira is an all-girls boarding and day school very similar to Wesley Girls, and it

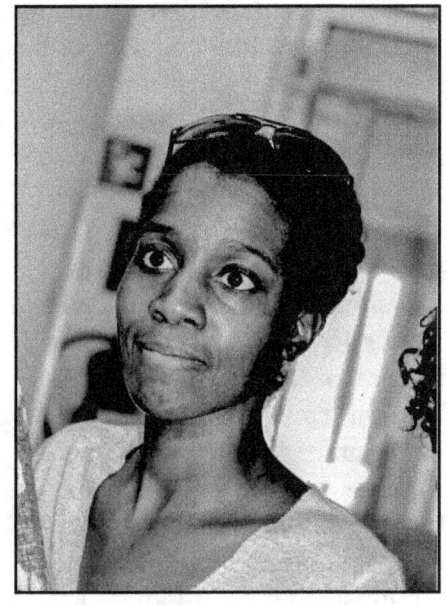

Awoye in New York City

turned out to be a vibrant and very enriching environment for her. We seemed to have made the right decisions on the children's education. Regarding Albert and my personal situation, however, it was very different. My hardworking established husband had been working in a pediatric practice in Princeton and New Brunswick, New Jersey, which he loved. I had lived alone in Rome with trans-Atlantic travel to see each other as often as we could manage. With my transfer to Namibia, however, we were faced with a decision. We had always been close so being apart from each other had been extremely difficult. We talked incessantly about it, continually weighing our options on what to do and how to make our separation work for the overall good of the family. I was in an organization I loved, doing exactly the kind of work I had always wanted to do. We were both so wrapped up in this dialogue it got to a point we were not sure what to do. We consulted with one of Albert's closest confidantes and lifelong friend, Professor Albert Fiadjoe, over a period of months, weighing all the pros and cons of Albert leaving what he loved to join me and embark on our global journey.

I spent a lot of time consulting with the Namibia Health regulatory bodies and UN colleagues on possible work options for Albert. As overwhelming as that turned out to be, I kept at it. After much angst and hesitation, Albert decided he would move to join me in Namibia so we would make the best of it. This was one of the hardest decisions we have had to make in our lives. We were now in unknown territory. Yes, a lot of families in the international community we knew were making such hard decisions, but one can never compare any two situations. Each family circumstance is unique and special and has its own dynamics to deal with. As much as we thought we had

Emefa at home in East Windsor

consulted and weighed all the possible options, we knew and felt deep down at the time that it would not be smooth sailing. We were committed to trying it since we decided living perpetually apart was not a good option for us.

During several travels to New Jersey, we sold our beloved home in West Windsor, consolidated our affairs, and moved together to Namibia. The new drama started. We were working on the assumption that with Namibia being newly independent with a dire need for physicians, it would not be a terribly difficult process for Albert to secure a position, even on a temporary basis. Naively, we believed that the chances for him to find clinical work that would be meaningful to him professionally would not be terribly difficult, especially since we would be in developing countries mostly that could use the services of a trained pediatrician from the United States. No matter who we spoke to they confirmed the need was there and it would not be a huge problem. Besides, other United Nations spouses were getting employed in different countries. All of that was true.

The crucial element we had not taken into consideration was the fact that my husband was very different from me and was not one to knock on every possible door looking for work. Having gone through extensive medical training, he had no doubt that he would find work, but he was not going to stoop to literally plead for work he was aptly qualified for. Given our personalities were so very different, I would generally be the one to push through the process on his behalf, talking to colleagues and strangers and making every effort to pave a path for him.

In Namibia after months of struggling and begging colleagues, he found a position within the United Nations system as a medical officer in the refugee camp near Okahandja, which was devoted to Angolan refugees fleeing the fighting in their home country. It was not what we had envisioned, but we had learned to be grateful for whatever came our way, mixing the good with the bad and the uncertain. Although he had to spend the week at the camp, he was home in Windhoek each weekend. Albert was truly a warm and loving physician; within no time he became an indispensable physician at the camp, often staying over on weekends and holidays to ensure that the health needs of the refugees were being adequately met. He advocated for increasing the nutritional rations being provided by The United Nations High Commissioner for Refugees (UNHCR) and worked closely with other UNHCR staff and the responsible Ministry of Health team in Windhoek to enhance the overall welfare of those at the camp, especially the camp's children.

In Namibia Albert and I were able to make his move and transition work reasonably well. We were surrounded by a new community of friends and colleagues. We formed a very close relationship with the small Ghanaian community that attended the same Methodist Church in downtown Windhoek, including Kwami and Mana Avafia, Akua and Kwesi Dua-Agyeman, Auntie Clara Donkor, and Elizabeth and NiiBoye Quaye. We would meet each Sunday after church in one person's house for an all-day lunch, building lifelong friendships. The critical need for community and love always seems to be the binding glue that helps one in life, no matter the circumstances. In Namibia this was again reinforced and nurtured. Over twenty years after we left Namibia these friends are still critical in our lives.

In moving from Namibia to other duty stations the challenges for Albert to secure work and be meaningfully engaged in his field of expertise persisted. In Ethiopia he obtained an assignment on the health desk at USAID and a couple of consultancies with PAHO in India. But besides that he could not and would not be able to adapt to the ever-changing need to look for work. Over time, in spite of our ability to manage the family on one income, travel, and do the things we both loved, he began to become periodically depressed. His enthusiasm and spirits were down, and I would often come home from my exciting day to find him glued to the television with absolutely no interest in anything else. He was not happy but, like the true trooper he was, he let everyone feel he was okay.

We spent time discussing perhaps the possibility of him returning to the United States to work since by then all the children were in school stateside. He was losing so much of his self-esteem and did not want to move back without me. I was at a loss in what to do and, as always, I would kick in trying for us to get some professional help with counseling to help direct us a bit on what to do. Albert had always been loving and good to me, and to see him waning and losing himself was extremely difficult. We were getting lost amid all the other good things that were happening to the family, especially with the children. The questions we struggled with were around whether we had made the wrong decision in having him leave his profession to move with me.

In hindsight we could see it had not worked out well for him, and that we did not have similar abilities to adapt to whatever changes came our way. Albert had gone through a very predictable life with everything falling in place for him. Adapting to negative change and forces was not something he had had to deal with, and now at an older age in foreign lands away from friends and other family he was feeling completely overwhelmed. In addition to professional support and ongoing conversations with some of his old friends around the world, it became clear how much he was struggling with life.

To compound this for him, during our stay in India at just about the time we were to be transferred to Geneva, he was diagnosed with a heart disease, which completely threw our lives apart. A routine annual physical at the AIIMS Hospital revealed a blockage in his heart, which needed immediate medical attention. My tears could not stop flowing. I was petrified. What was happening to my husband? I was not sure what to do. However, the Indian doctors were excellent. They reassured me that it was a disease that could be taken care of with surgery. They provided us with all the necessary test records we needed. After a brief stop in Geneva we headed off to New York Presbyterian Hospital in Manhattan for a second opinion.

I have always dreaded disease and sickness and was desperate to ensure Albert had the best treatment possible. Through the international referral and support office at New York Presbyterian, Dr. Campagna, a wonderful cardiologist, became Albert's doctor. All possible diagnostics tests were carried out and, in consultation with other cardiologists at the hospital, it was confirmed that Albert had a major blockage in one of his heart arteries and needed immediate bypass surgery. This was major surgery even in my layperson's mind, and I was beside myself with fear.

With the support of close friends and family and Dr. Campagna's unrelenting assurances, I calmed down enough and believed it would go well. The surgery took place in September 2003, and after an extensive period of convalescing Albert was well enough for us to go back to Geneva for me to start work. We could not have been at a better place during this phase in our lives.

Switzerland with its natural beauty, serene landscape, and slow organized pace was perfect for convalescing. The ten-thousand-dollar deposit we had put down for an apartment through a rental agent became a nightmare as he turned out to be a scoundrel and had disappeared with our money and a lot of other people's rental money. In spite of the hiccup, we were able to quickly find a nice apartment in the village of Founex amid the wine fields in the countryside, just a twenty-minute drive to work in Geneva. Sitting in our small dining room one could see the French Alps through the French doors rising on the other side of Lake Geneva. When we lifted our eyes outside we would see the grape fields starting at the end of our lawn, leading to the Nyon-Geneva train tracks at the edge of the lake. It was such a wonderful location, and I would always comment on how calming the humming of the trains passing through was for me. Over time Albert got progressively better; his spirits lifted again, and he was able to enjoy himself again.

Albert made a real sacrifice for me, leaving his prestigious and comfortable position to give me the opportunities I thrived on. What he did was brave and groundbreaking and, in reality, what many women were doing for their husbands, not the other way around. This was more so for a Ghanaian man. It was unheard of. It was groundbreaking, and I appreciated him tremendously.

With each challenge we faced over the years, the Timpo Five was able to galvanize together and carve a path forward. We would count our blessings and our joys and try to learn from the hardships we had endured.

With my move to work in New York we were all finally back together living in New Jersey, settled in East Windsor, just eleven miles from our old home in West Windsor.

Emelia at retirement

EPILOGUE

The Ghanaian adage of the importance of a village in raising a child is as true now as it was centuries ago. Having people around you from an early age who affirm you as an important part of society regardless of your skills or deficiencies has been so critical to my growth and upbringing.

It has been a very circuitous journey, and through it all the groundedness I feel in all I do goes back to my childhood at Suame. Hard work was expected so getting up at dawn as a child to walk to New Suame to fetch a bucket of water before having a shower or going back for more for Maa to have water to cook was nothing but a fun expedition because we would always do these chores as a group of family, neighbors and strangers alike.

After years of hard work, ensuring I was putting out the very best work I could do throughout my career, I could sense the unease and dwindling interest in coping any longer with the inequalities and discrimination within the work environment. Coupled with the toll the four-hour commutes to New York City were taking on me, I literally jumped at the optional retirement packages that were offered to staff as a way to reduce the bloated staffing of UNAIDS. At the time I joined UNAIDS there were close to two hundred and fifty staff globally, a family environment in which innovative thinking, hard work, and collaborative effort were appreciated. The organization had now more than twelve thousand staff members with numerous consultancies carved out for friends and relations; the politics were completely overtaking the needs of the communities we were meant to serve. I was ready to leave, and the opportunity landed on my lap.

Through all my career, discrimination and inequities have been prevalent. I survived it all because I operated on the basis of ensuring I was making the best of every opportunity offered. I trusted in the competence and contributions of my staff and everyone I encountered. My grandmother's perpetual saying of "knowledge is not in one person's head" has been my mantra. No matter what the circumstances, all the people I interacted with had come to realize that I would always work with whoever and I would always voice my opinion as warranted, believing I was not in meetings as an observer but as an integral part of any team.

I would voice openly any concerns I saw on discriminatory practices to colleagues and bosses alike. Justice had to prevail no matter what. Yes, at times I could sense the resentment to my voicing openly the wrongs inflicted on other minority colleagues. It was my duty to do so, and I did not shirk from it. I also know that due to my being vocal in openly discussing these discriminatory practices, I was not recognized for certain advancement opportunities, but I was comfortable with it. I understood the landscape and the internal politics of management and senior leaders. Anyone interested in paying attention to the inequities in the system could see it clearly on many fronts. I had served my time, made enormous contributions to the system, my family had benefited immensely, and at that point I did not have any more energy to expend. I was ready to retire. On 30 September 2012 I packed my bags from my New York City office, said my final goodbyes to colleagues and friends, and have never looked back.

It has indeed been a blessing to have my three daughters. They have been at the core of my being and my life, and I would not have had it any other way. One would think that with all the moving the family had to do as a result of my work with the United Nations, they would have been grumpy and make it even more difficult with each move and its related challenges. Instead, they have been a wonderful team throughout, with all the difficulties and opportunities that the new lifestyle had presented.

With the initial move to Ghana there was the most apprehension. We were all so attached to our home at 4 Aldrich Way. They had their friends, their sporting and Girl Scouts groups, their music programs, and all the fun they were having with friends. It was not an easy decision. However, having heard so much about Ghana and having had a wonderful time during our family visits, it did not sound as a foreign place. They knew the family; their pampering Granma would be there, and yes, they would make new friends. As it turned out they settled in well at the British School of Lomé in Togo. In fact, they thrived, made new friends, and were happy to be immersed in the French language.

I recall when Emefa had wanted to learn Spanish in Middle School at the West Windsor School district. The guidance counselors suggested she should take art instead. Of course, I had to make an appointment and go to the principal's office to have a long talk with both the teacher and the principal. As far as I was concerned every student should be required to take a language course whether they also did art or something else. Eventually, she was allowed to be in the Spanish class. It was refreshing to be in an environment where having fluency in a second language was encouraged for all.

Moving from one duty station to another meant that I became an expert in planning and organizing flights around the world. Carlson Wagonlit was initially the travel company for FAO. All the staff became close friends, considering the amount of time I was spending with them to plan holiday trips in Rome, Namibia, and elsewhere with Awoye at Ohio Wesleyan, Emefa at Philips Exeter and later Cornell, and Edem at the Madeira School in Maclean, Virginia, and later at medical school in Dublin, Ireland.

This is how family travel traditions were developed. We made it a regular feature to organize trips for the Timpo Five to go out sightseeing the highlights of the country where we would be stationed when the girls came home on holidays. We all loved Rome; with the girls we would visit Venice, Pompeii, Florence, and Castel Gondolfo, a mere fifteen miles from my new apartment in the Fioranello area outside the city belt parkway. These were marvelous times. We were happy, content, and made space for each other's interests.

Such excursions were repeated in every duty station. It was all mesmerizing. Awoye decided to major in theatre, Spanish, and French. She did very well in Ohio and followed it up with an intensive French master's degree at the University of London branch based in Paris. Prior to Paris Albert and I were thoroughly and pleasantly surprised when Awoye with three friends from Ohio Wesleyan decided to take a year off after graduation and spend the time in Ghana and the West Africa region in general. She felt very comfortable with the life and people of Ghana and was able to explore parts of the country I had not even been, the northern and upper regions of Ghana and beyond where the people and cultures were very different from that in the southern part of the country.

Albert and I were very apprehensive about a career in theatre.

What did we know? How can you take care of yourself when you are working as a freelancer with long periods between assignments and having to work in restaurants and take other temporary not well-paid jobs to fill the gap? Coming from an environment in which you had to be a doctor, lawyer, or engineer above all else, it was difficult to understand. We had a long learning curve. At the back of my mind, though, I kept thinking it was best for her to make her own path in an area of interest to her. Who knows how she will end up? Awoye had always been hardworking and tenacious so I felt no matter what she decided to do she would put her mind to it. With her calm and reflective composure, she was admired everywhere she went and by whoever she worked with. With her impeccable writing skills, she was able to get consulting editing opportunities with UNICEF between her theater assignments. It was difficult at the beginning but over time she has done well in the theater industry as a director in her own right. With her wonderful mentor, Reuben Santiago-Hudson, and others, she is blossoming and doing very well and is recognized nationally within her field.

Emefa and her dad spent one summer exploring colleges while I was in Rome. After visiting Georgetown in Washington, DC, and the University of Pennsylvania in Philadelphia, there was a last-minute dash to see Cornell University in Ithaca. She applied to a number of colleges and was thrilled to be accepted into Cornell with a major in economics. She was following me to my alma mater, which had a very special place in my heart. As is common with young ones these days, it did not take long for Emefa to change her major to government and film studies as her second year approached. Ithaca is such a beautiful place, and she settled in and thrived.

After Cornell, however, she was not quite sure what to do next. Luckily for her, by that time Albert and I were based in Switzerland. Emefa decided to come spend some time in Geneva with us and possibly attend a graduate school there. She found short-term employment with the Global Fund for AIDS, TB and Malaria in their grants management division working with different countries as they submitted grant proposals for funding. That assignment and her immersion within the international area increased her interest in pursuing a master's degree in public policy. With my term in Switzerland coming to an end and the high cost of living there,

Emefa opted to come back to the United States and pursue her degree at Rutgers. She has since gone on to do significant work in the burgeoning field of data privacy and contracts in working with numerous international companies.

Edem has had the most transitions. When I initially moved to Rome, I had hoped to take Edem with me from Ghana after my initial settling in period. After much research with colleagues in Rome, I found an excellent international school, Mary Mount School, which in my mind would have been perfect for Edem. She would not hear of it, did not want to go to the school, and preferred the Jack and Jill in Ghana. After many difficult discussions and arguments, we decided it was best for her to finish at Jack and Jill and then transfer to the British School where Awoye and Emefa were. She loved that idea so that was exactly what we did. There was peace.

After Awoye and Emefa left BSL and I was transferred to Namibia, we thought it best for her to move to Namibia with me. At least she would be in a stable school environment for at least three to four years, by which time it may be easier for her to transition to a high school in the United States. Windhoek International School (WIS) turned out to be a godsend for Edem. She loved it and was doing very well in all her classes; above all, she had our good family friend Mrs. Mana Avafia, who was a long-term teacher at the school, to keep an eye on her and mentor her. She has lifelong friends from WIS all over the world with children whose families were also within the diplomatic community as well as local Namibians. Being a small school in a rather small capital city of just over two hundred thousand people, Edem had a busy social calendar with her friends.

All good things though must come to an end. My desire to stay in Namibia for at least four years was not to be once I received my posting to UNAIDS Ethiopia as the focal point to the African Union, among other responsibilities. At this point there was no question Edem had to go back to the United States. After extensive research we decided it was best for her to attend the Madeira School in MacLean, Virginia, on the outskirts of Washington, DC. After visiting the school we discovered that it had all the elements of the nurturing and yet demanding environment as Wesley Girls High

School. We felt it would be a good fit; again, it turned out to be the best place for her for the last three years of high school.

With weekly Wednesday internships on Capitol Hill in the office of Representative Javier Barcera of California as well as another internship with an accomplished photographer in Washington, DC, and continuation of her piano lessons to an advanced level, no one was sure if Edem would still be interested in medical school. That had been her dream from a very young age but with all the other interests she had we were not sure. She was, however, determined to pursue medicine and then shocked us by looking to complete a degree in medicine so she could go directly to medical school from high school as is done in most parts of the world, as opposed to finishing a baccalaureate degree first. We did find a direct program in Wake Forest University but eventually she decided on the option at the Royal College of Surgeons in Dublin, Ireland. So off we went to Dublin. With her big uncle K.O.P. and his wife, Carol, in Belfast, she was never far from family. They surrounded her with love, and with our periodic visits over the six-year period Edem was there, it also gave all of us the chance to grow even closer to them.

The lives of Awoye, Emefa, and Edem have been a real whirlwind just as it was for me and Albert. We all tried to make it work. Global travel opportunities, learning, and growth were immense for all of us. In the end, though, what they missed was the stability of growing up in a few places and making strong friends and developing relationships. There were no proms or looking for dates, and no strong relationships with other young Ghanaian Americans their age.

The families and friends we had when they were young had also dispersed across the country, and there were very few opportunities to hang out with their children in the long years that we were out of the country. In hindsight I always think that if Maa had lived longer, she would have seen that aspect of young girls growing up and helped to create other opportunities for stability. I am sure if we had to do it again it would be a little different. But overall, they have each in their own unique way grown up to be highly accomplished, bright, caring, and loving ladies, and we are blessed to see who they have all become.

ACKNOWLEDGMENTS

This has been a long journey, and it would not have come to fruition without a lot of handholding and support from a range of people. My husband, Albert, had always encouraged me to write my life story, which led me to start writing before he passed away. I am forever grateful to him.

Thanks to Professor Kofi Darkwa for his initial editing of the manuscript and to Karen Hodges Miller and her team for their invaluable insights in editing and sharpening the script especially for people who may not be familiar with any Ghanaian culture and norms. I thank Eric Labacz for his graphic design of the cover, which we all loved at first sight. I am grateful to Alex Archine and Victor Essien for their willingness to read and edit the initial draft. I thank Barbara Fox for her insightful feedback and edits and guidance on finding editors to work with. I also thank my many friends and family who helped me along the way, sharing memories of events and names long forgotten, especially Conrad Bonsi, Mohammed Chambas, Vicky Wireko, Nora Osafo, Minnette Halm, Ohenese Apau Sakyi, Cynthia Poku, and Ophelia Mensah.

To my constant partners—my dear daughters Awoye, Emefa, and Edem—for working with me each step of the way, making suggestions, editing each draft, and sorting out the myriad family photos as needed. I am forever indebted to them for their love, unfailing support, and willingness to do whatever it takes.

Finally, I give thanks to numerous friends and loved ones who encouraged me in various ways through the years to bring this work to fruition.

www.ingramcontent.com/pod-product-compliance
Lightning Source LLC
Chambersburg PA
CBHW060519130626
46553CB00002B/569